Applied Harmony

by

Carolyn A. Alchin

Revised, and with additional chapters
by

Vincent Jones, Ph.D.

PROFESSOR OF EDUCATION
(MUSIC EDUCATION DEPARTMENT)
New York University

Part I

Diatonic Harmony and Simple Modulation

Price $4.50
in U.S.A.

HIGHLAND MUSIC COMPANY
1311 N. Highland Avenue, Hollywood 28, California

ACKNOWLEDGMENTS

The author is indebted to the following publishers for per-
mission to use exerpts from copyrighted works: G. Schirmer,
New York; Oliver Ditson Co., Boston; Novello Publishing Co.,
London, for the excerpts from Elgar's "Dream of Gerontius;"
Durand & Co., Paris, for those from "Pelleas et Melisande;"
Arthur Schmidt, of Boston, for those of MacDowell.

Foreword.

The purpose of this book is to provide a course of study that will be simple, direct, and from the outset insure a musical understanding and mastery of the material of music; a course that will teach the *nature* of music, and through that, lessen the burden of rules and their long train of exceptions; a course that will cultivate the imagination with the technical development; that will awaken and increase a love and appreciation for the best in music; a course that will be *related to all branches of music education and of practical value* in every line of music study.

There is a constant appeal to the *ear* and *feeling*. Thought without feeling is too cold. Feeling without thought can not be intelligently expressed. The highest musicianship results from a union of thought and feeling. The late Judge Troward said: "Thought creates form, but it is feeling that gives vitality to thought. Thought without feeling may be constructive, but it can never be creative." *

Mozart said: "Melody is the essence of music." Since there is no melody without rhythm and harmonic regulation, *music*, then, *is the union of rhythm and tone*, and the intelligent study of music is a study of these relations.

Our first work in cultivating the feeling for relationship and its resultant qualities in key is through the principle of "Tonal Magnetism," a relationship that is the product of nature. From the relationship of tones in scale and tones in chord, we pass to the relationship of chords in key, their relationship to accent and rhythm, and the relationship of keys. *Rhythm is a vital factor in the selection of harmonies.*

The material is introduced progressively and in the order most frequently and naturally used. As each new factor is presented, the student is first made familiar with it by an abundance of excerpts from the works of the best composers—both old and new—from which one sees the various relations of the new material and the practical application of the few necessary rules that are given.

The *analysis* is *followed* by *synthesis* through patterns for keyboard work, the use of the new material in the harmonization of melodies, and lastly, original work embodying the new material. An ounce of application is worth a pound of theory.

The late Julius Klauser (to whom I am greatly indebted for his splendid instruction) first drew my attention to this principle of relationship and the importance of working from the melodic basis. In his book, "The Nature of Music," he says: "Melody is the direct reporter of fundamentals and chords. Fundamentals and chords are not reporters of melody, though they may suggest them. It is a psychological error to suppose that any beginner, however gifted, possesses the perceptive power to grasp the four-voice music-

* *The Dore Lectures.*

thought embodied in given basses. The impossible being demanded, the student's performance is necessarily mechanical and musically dead, since his musical faculties are not called into requisition. * * * Melody being the one simple and real fact in the beginner's inner consciousness and experience of music, it follows that the given melody is the one thing that his musical faculties can seize upon and be stirred by, the one thing that lies within his intellectual grasp and appreciation, the one thing that he appreciates and remembers as a whole, and in relation to which it is easy for him to add something else, since it explains the musical what, how and why of the addition. * * *

"Exercises in the given bass, owing to their arbitrary prescription of the order and arrangement of material, completely cut off the student from that independence of thought and judgment in the use and selection of chord-material which is so essential to its mastery. Given a melody to harmonize, the student sets out with the one thing he can mentally grasp; he perfectly comprehends the subject of his work and therefore also his object. Having a tangible subject he has a tangible object; his melody is his preceptor and guide in his choice of harmonies."

The melodies contained in this work have been chosen with a view of developing taste, also to provide every difficulty one is likely to meet in creative work. While original work is required at all stages of study, until a student can write as well or as correctly as the composers from whose works these melodies have been taken, it will be well to use more of the best models. Unless otherwise stated, the excerpts by Debussy are taken from the opera "Pelleas et Melisande." All of those by Elgar are taken from his "Dream of Gerontius."

It would be unreasonable to expect a work of this nature to be without defects. The perfect text-book will be written when the perfect teacher appears. There are some teachers who seem to think that they will be condemned for lack of originality if they use a text-book. As a result, there is much valuable time lost in dictation, and the student is at a disadvantage because he does not always remember what has been given to him in the all too brief lesson period. There is no new music material, but there are new combinations and rhythmic settings to be discovered. There are largely increasing numbers of people who want to compose, and their futile attempts bring us to a realization of the fact that they need training in *musical effects*, rather than arbitrary rules that make little or no appeal to the music sense. Broad, basic principles are needed at every step. A system that leaves nothing for the student to discover and no opportunity to exercise discrimination *does not educate*.

Experience has proven that with this system desired results are acquired in less time and without hampering the freedom of expression by the many prohibitions. Through the appeal to the nature of the music material, the affirmative principle prevails; the students become *discriminating musicians*, not mathematicians.

CAROLYN A. ALCHIN.

Los Angeles, California.

PREFACE TO REVISED EDITIONS

The revised editions of APPLIED HARMONY have appeared as a result of requests from former students of the late Carolyn Alchin and from teachers who did not have the opportunity of studying under her inspiring guidance.

The basic features of the original text are retained and it is hoped that the philosophy and spirit which animated the author are present in the revisions. Carolyn Alchin was one of the most musicianly and progressively-minded teachers of harmony in the country. Her unusual perception of the *reasons* underlying harmonic relationships and her sensitivity to the *musical* aspect of teaching these relationships caused her to evolve a methodology far in advance of the systems prevalent in her day. She clarified harmonic procedures in a practical but also in an aesthetic manner. Many current practices in the teaching of harmony can be traced to her influence.

The material of Part I (Diatonic Harmony and Modulation to Closely Related Keys) has been re-arranged in order to aid in more practical class presentation. The first two chapters of the original text have been expanded and may be employed as a brief course in elementary theory.

The APPENDIX (added in 1935) includes chapters on Consecutive First Inversions; Secondary Seventh Chords and a discussion of the Figured Bass. Although Miss Alchin did not approach the study of harmony from the figured bass, it seemed advisable to include a discussion of this method of figuring so that students might be able to understand and work out basses from compositions of the periods when that system of figuring was common. Since the original text emphasized the stylistic aspect of harmony, the inclusion of the figured bass seems justified as part of the historical evolution of harmony, even though the present author does not advocate that approach in the introduction of harmonic problems.

In the present revision the APPENDIX has been retained but the explanation of the figured bass has been introduced early in the text. Another system of figuring, widely used, has also been included so that students may employ the three methods interchangeably as they pursue their study. New exercises have been added which combine melody harmonization with figured bass (in the same exercise).

In the chapters on intervals there are many examples from contemporary music, including excerpts from leading American composers. The author believes that there is no reason to postpone analysis of the contemporary idiom, in its relation to intervals, until the student is advanced. The latter is usually more interested in compositions of the present day than in examples from earlier periods.

Many new suggestions for harmonization of melodies in the text have been added, employing notation rather than explanation.

A novel addition in Chapter XIX is a "minature survey" of techniques used in composition from 1600 to the present. Most of the exercises are based on works of the master composers. There are several exercises which employ triads as used by contemporary composers. The student need not defer study of such techniques until he has mastered chromatic harmony and therefore they are included in the text. The student who has carefully worked out the exercises of the "survey" should be able to compose in the smaller forms, employing the harmonic material made available in the text.

It is hoped that the re-arrangement of material and the many additions will widen the scope of the text and enrich the pedagogical aspect.

The author of the revisions is indebted to Bertha Wingert Bailey, Mrs. Julia Howell Oversheiner and the late Miss Doris E. Moon for valuable suggestions and assistance in working out the material in high school and college classes.

The author is particularly grateful to Miss Nancy Campbell for invaluable aid in the preparation of the present revision.

VINCENT JONES.

New York City
1958

TABLE OF CONTENTS

Introduction.

Prerequisite Knowledge for the Student.

It is assumed that the student is familiar with the following:

1. The treble and bass staves; the G and F clefs.

2. The significance of duration values as expressed by ○, 𝅝, 𝅘𝅥, 𝅘𝅥𝅮, 𝅘𝅥𝅯, etc.

3. The significance of pitch names as expressed by the sharp (♯), the flat (♭) the double-sharp (✕), the double flat (♭♭), the natural or cancel sign (♮).

4. Knowledge of pitch names as represented on the piano; the location of whole steps and half steps.

To the Teacher.

Distribution of Material.

This text is designed to meet the demands of both high school and college students. For that reason, certain chapters contain supplementary material of more advanced grade. Most of the chapters contain short and easy melodies followed by a section of longer and more difficult melodies. The average high school class need not do all of the exercises. The teacher who is in sympathy with modern educational theory and practice believes in *maximum* and *minimum* assignments to meet the needs of *individuals*.

This text is not arranged in a definite number of lessons, because each teacher has a different problem to meet. Chapters I-V can be used as a course in elementary theory. For students who have had little musical experience, this work may cover at least one semester. Chapters VI-XIII, covering primary harmonies, represent another semester of work. The remaining chapters which cover secondary chords and simple modulation may occupy a semester. College students may use the text for first year work, leaving the second year for chromatic harmony and advanced modulation. Additional melodies for harmonization and material for melodic and harmonic dictation are contained in "Tone Thinking and Ear Testing" by Carolyn Alchin.

Presentation of Material.

(1) *New material* should always be introduced *aurally* and correlated *immediately* with selections known to the student or compositions which will later be used for analysis. This text endeavors to introduce each new problem in this manner, but no book can take the place of a skillful teacher in the first presentation of subject matter.

(2) *The appreciative element* is of supreme importance. The student should gain an appreciation of the *effect* of chords, their characteristic "color," their use in actual composition etc. The sections on *analysis* provide an abundance of material. This aspect of harmony is often neglected but it is the phase which will remain when *facts* are forgotten. No teacher should be satisfied with *skill* and *factual knowledge* only.

(3) *Keyboard practice* is necessary; two or three pupils can play the scale drills and various interval sequences at the same time. When two pianos are available, one pupil may play a chord accompaniment on one piano while a second pupil extemporizes a melody over the chord pattern at the second piano. This can also be done at one piano. The ensemble training is valuable in itself, aside from the harmonic drill.

(4) In the text suggestions are given to aid in harmonizing the melodies. The teacher should write one or two measures which will serve as a model. For example: the suggestion relative to No. 3 of Ex. 91, page 53. The discussion is found on page 52.

Example.  etc.

(5) *Melody-writing to words* is important but is not included in the body of the text, because a teacher should first *direct this work in class.* In setting even a simple stanza the following principles operate:

(a) Scan the words; determine the general measure, as: $\frac{2}{4}, \frac{4}{4}, \frac{3}{4}, \frac{6}{8},$ etc.

(b) Represent the stanza in rhythmic notation. Be sure the metrical and musical accents agree.

(c) The mood of the poem will suggest the general melodic line, whether scale line or skips.

(d) There should be at least one *focal point* in every song. Even short songs contain a climax of some sort.

(e) Avoid repeating the same tone on many accents.

(f) Certain words suggest upward skips, other words suggest skips downward.

(g) Avoid emphasis of unimportant words. Do not place them on accents or on high tones. Ordinarily, words of a single syllable should not be divided

as: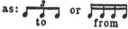

(h) Analysis of the best material in the various school song books will teach the pupil more than any number of rules.

The following CORRECTION CHART (*footnote) will prove valuable in correcting papers. Errors may be marked by number. The pupil refers to the chart for his corrections.

Example.

CORRECTION CHART.

1. Law of Tonal Magnetism.
2. Chord Spelling.
   (a) Add 7th.
   (b) Add 9th.
3. Chord position.
   (a) Too strong.
   (b) Too weak.
4. Principle of color against basic.
5. Harmonic Progression.
   (a) Anticipation across the bar line (Harmonic syncopation.)
   (b) Treat soprano as chord tone.
   (c) Treat soprano as bytone.
6. Doubling.
7. Spacing.
   (a) Overlapping of voices.
   (b) Reverse voices to give correct spacing.
   (c) Register.
8. Direction of voices.
9. Omit.
10. Awkward.

* Chart by Doris E. Moon.

ADDITIONAL SUGGESTIONS FOR THE APPRECIATIVE
ASPECT OF HARMONY

The text includes many excerpts from music literature of all periods which can be used to give the student a wider and deeper appreciation of the stylistic phase of harmony, beyond the mere technical discussion of problems in writing. Some specific references follow:

Excellent examples of perfect fourths and fifths appear in such divergent compositions as: Hindemith, *Third Piano Sonata;* Samuel Barber, *Piano Sonata,* Op. 26; Bartok, *Three Burlesques,* No. 1; Menotti, *The Medium* (the scene where Monica sings "Mother, mother, are you there?") and page 68 of the same score. Interesting passages of fourths occur in the Scherzo and the Finale of Vaughan Williams' *Symphony in F minor.* The "Brindisi" from Verdi's *Otello* (Act I) and the final duet from Giordano's *Andrea Chenier* (Act IV) demonstrate dramatic usage of perfect fourths. Passages consisting entirely of minor thirds are found in Movement II of Hindemith's *Third Piano Sonata.* There is a melody in Prokofiev's *Love for Three Oranges* (page 179 of the score) which employs major thirds almost exclusively.

The text introduces the I and V7 harmonies by means of Beethoven's First Symphony (see page 40). Attention may be called to the fact that Beethoven uses the same two harmonies in later works such as the Piano Sonata, Op. 111 and the Adagio from the String Quartet, Op. 135. The composer found these chords sufficient to project the lofty musical ideas of his later works as well as those of an earlier period.

In the chapter on the Supertonic (page 120) there are numerous examples in the material for analysis on page 125. The supertonic chord can be introduced through number 1 from Ex. 184 (page 125) by playing a recording of Elisabeth's aria, "Dich Theure Halle" from Wagner's Tannhauser and noting the music which follows the close of the aria. The excerpt in the text appears at this point and is excellent since the supertonic harmony "presides" during four full measures.

Note that the introduction of the Submediant harmony (page 133) is accomplished through a passage from Handel's *Messiah,* in which the aesthetic aspect is stressed rather than strictly technical. Such a teaching procedure will arouse and maintain interest more than a mere discussion of the construction of the chord.

The Mediant harmony may be introduced by playing a recording of the third movement of Brahms' Fourth Symphony. The opening is then played on the piano, the mediant chord is discovered and discussed in relation to its quality (minor) and its resolution to the IV. In this type of approach the mediant harmony is treated more in the nature of a "musical event" than a fact to be learned.

In discussing the Moussorgsky excerpt from Ex. 201 (page 146) the teacher may call attention to the fact that the composer was greatly influenced by Russian church music and folk song when he wrote *Boris Godunov.*

The above suggestions may be applied to almost all the examples for analysis in this text, and additional material, plus suggestions for its use, will be found in the author's *Essentials in the Teaching of Harmony.*

Chapter I.

Fundamental Intervals. Development of key-feeling.

Experiment I.

Ex. 1.

play   sing

Experiment with Ex. 1(a) as indicated. Play the first two bars, sing the next three notes, and when you have established the rhythm, supply a tone in bar 4. Do not think a particular tone but allow the voice to follow its natural inclination. Compare your result with that shown at (b).

The relationship existing between these two tones is called an *interval*. An *interval* is the relation of any two tones with respect to their difference in pitch. On the staff this relation appears as their distance apart.

Count the staff degrees (lines and spaces) in this interval, counting the lowest note as a degree. The general name of this interval is *octave*, as there are eight staff degrees involved, the word *octave* meaning eight. The octave is also called "perfect" as this is the most perfect relationship that can exist between two tones.

Listening Drill.

1. Sing the first two phrases of "Annie Laurie" and discover the octave.

2. Sing the first two phrases of "Swanee River" and note the octave skip.

3. If possible hear a record of the Bach-Gounod "Ave Maria" and note where the octave skips occur.

4. Play, or have someone play, the Wagner excerpt. Listen for the interval of an octave. This melody occurs at the opening of the second act of "Die Walküre" and is sung by Brunnhilde. It is the "call" by which she summons her sister Valkyries. What effect is given by the leap of an octave?

Ex. 2.

Singing Drills.

1. Sing the octave from many pitches. Sing both tones, always singing from an unaccented pulse to an accented pulse, as

2. Play the lower tone and sing the upper.

3. Play the upper tone and sing the lower.

Keyboard Practice.

1. Starting with middle C, play octaves on every key as shown:

Ex. 3.   etc

Note that the octave is from a white key to a white key, and from a black key to a black key in all cases.

2. Play Ex. 3 in higher and lower registers on the piano and start on different pitches.

Writing Drills.

1. Write octaves on the staff, using both clefs, and starting on various pitches. Observe that if the lower note is on a line the upper note is on a space and vice versa. If the lower note is on a line, count to the fourth space above and place the upper note in that space. If the lower note is in a space, count to the 4th line above and place the upper note on that line. If the lower note is a sharp, the upper note will be a sharp. The same principle applies to flats.

2. Write the keyboard sequence *away* from the piano.

Experiment II.

Ex. 4.

Tap the rhythm of Ex. 4(a). After establishing the rhythm, sing what is written and preserve the rhythm of measure three but do not sing anything in that measure. Repeat several times. Now sing thru and supply the tone which seems to be demanded in measure three. Compare your result with that shown at (b). Count the staff degrees in the new interval shown at (c). This interval is called a *fifth* as it contains five degrees. It is also called "perfect" and is the next most perfect relationship existing between two tones, after the octave.

Listening Drill.

1. Play or have someone play the example from Handel's "Messiah." Where do you hear the interval of a perfect fifth?

2. Play or have someone play "The Swan" of Saint-Saëns. Sing the melody and recognize the interval of a fifth.

Ex. 5.

What is the character of the perfect fifth? Used melodically it is usually strong. When the tones are sounded together the effect is hollow.

Singing Drills.

1. Sing perfect fifths from different pitches. Sing from an unaccented to an accented pulse. Sing both the fifth *above* and the fifth *below*.

2. Play the lower tone and sing the upper.

3. Play the upper tone and sing the lower.

Keyboard Practice.

1. Starting on middle C, play a perfect fifth above every white key. The fifth above will be a white key in every case except when you reach b. The perfect fifth above b is f♯.

2. Starting on c♯ (or d♭) play a perfect fifth above every black key. The fifth above will be a black key until you reach b♭. The perfect fifth above b♭ is f.

Summary. Perfect fifths occur from white to white keys and from black to black keys except on b and b♭.

3. Play the following sequence (a sequence is a figure or motive repeated on different degrees). Continue it until you reach the octave above the starting point. Observe the pattern carefully before playing; say the letter names of each interval just before playing it. Repeat the sequence until it is automatic.

4. Start the sequence on different pitches and play in higher and lower registers.

Ex. 6. etc.

Writing Drills.

1. From various pitches sing perfect fifths on "la" or neutral syllable, then on letter names and write on the staff while singing. Employ both clefs.

In writing note the following points:

a) A fifth is from a line to the second line above or from a space to the second space above.

b) On the staff all fifths are perfect except on b. This must be written b to f♯.

c) If the lower note of a perfect fifth is a sharp (♯) the upper note will be a sharp (♯). The perfect fifth above b♯ is f × (f double sharp).

d) If the lower note of a perfect fifth is a flat (♭) the upper note will be a flat (♭), except on b♭ (b♭ to f).

2. Write the sequence of the keyboard drill on the staff, *away* from the piano.

Experiment III.

Return to Experiment II and notice the interval created by the last two notes of (b).

Count the staff degrees contained in this interval.   It is called a *fourth* as there are four degrees. It is also called "perfect" and is the last of the series of perfect intervals.

When the fourth is played as a harmonic interval (the tones sounded together) it is similar to the fifth in its hollow quantity.

Listening Drill.

1. Sing "Flow Gently, Sweet Afton" and note the use of the perfect fourth.

2. Play or have someone play the following examples. Listen for the interval of the perfect fourth. In example No. 7(a) the fourth is particularly expressive of the words "I know." There is a sense of finality because of the relation of the tones in key (5 to 8).

Ex. 7.

I know that my Re-deem-er liv-eth

3. Compare the perfect fifth and the perfect fourth in the following examples. Notice that the effect is usually vigorous.

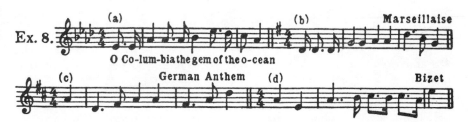

O Co-lum-bia the gem of the o-cean

Fifths and fourths when sung harmonically (the tones sounded together) are not especially pleasing. Music in medieval days was composed largely of those intervals, as they were considered the most perfect from a scientific standpoint. The music was monotonous and lacking in color. In piano and orchestral music, modern composers use these intervals for characteristic or descriptive effects. Try a succession of fifths in a low register on the piano. They suggest the desert and impart an atmosphere of gloom. In a higher register they suggest bells. Fourths also are used for bell effects and are found in Chinese music.

Sing a perfect fifth as at (a) Ex. 9. Sing the lower tone an octave higher as at (b). What interval results?

The process of placing the lower tone of an interval *above* the upper tone or placing the upper tone *below* the lower tone is called *inversion*. Perfect intervals remain perfect after being inverted. The theme from "The Flying Dutchman" of Wagner is an excellent example of the perfect fourth and its inversion the perfect fifth (c).

Singing Drills.

1. Sing perfect 4ths on various pitches. Sing from an unaccented to an accented pulse. Sing both the 4th above and the 4th below.

2. Play the lower tone and sing the upper.

3. Play the upper tone and sing the lower.

Keyboard Practice.

1. Starting on middle C, play a perfect 4th above every white key. The 4th above will be a white key in every case except when you reach f. The perfect 4th above f is b♭.

2. Starting on c♯ (or d♭) play a perfect 4th above every black key. The 4th above will be a black key in every case until you reach f♯. The perfect 4th above f♯ is b.

3. Play the following sequence and continue it until you reach the octave below the starting point. Observe the pattern carefully before playing; say the letter names of each interval just before playing. Repeat until the playing is automatic.

Ex. 10.   etc.

4. Start the sequence on different pitches and play it in higher and lower registers.

Writing Drills.

1. Follow the same procedure as for 5ths. Note the following points:

a) A fourth is from a line to the second space above or from a space to the second line above.

b) On the staff all 4ths are perfect except on f. This must be written f-b♭.

c) If the lower note of a perfect 4th is a sharp (♯) the upper note will be a sharp (♯) except at f♯.

d) If the lower note of a perfect 4th is a flat (♭) the upper note will be a flat (♭). The perfect 4th above f♭ is b♭♭. (b double flat.)

2. Write the keyboard sequence on the staff *away* from the piano.

Development of Key-feeling.

The three intervals discovered, when combined rhythmically, create melodies. The tones are so related to each other that they establish what is called a key. A group of tones related to one principal or fundamental tone constitutes a *key*. We have discovered only two of these tones, but they make a definite impression on the mind and are sufficient to create a musical phrase. The first tone is called the *tonic* and all the other tones are related to it. The perfect fifth above the tonic is named the *dominant* and next to the tonic, is the dominating tone of the key group.

Exercise I.

Take any pitch as *tonic*. Call it one (1) or the syllable "do".

Sing the perfect 5th above and call it five (5) or "so."

Call the octave above the tonic eight (8) or "do."

Note: When 5 appears with a line above it (as 5̄) that 5 is *below* 1. Otherwise 5 is above 1.

Sing all of the following groups to the rhythm of ♩♩|♩| and ♩♩|♩.|

(a)   1   5   1   (e)   1   1 |5   5|5̄   5̄|1 ‖

(b)   1   5̄   1   (f)   1   5|1   1|5̄   5̄|1 ‖

(c)   1   5   8

(d)   8   5   1

Exercise II.

Write all the groups of Ex. I on the staff on different pitches, using chromatic signs (sharps and flats) when necessary. Employ both clefs. At first, sing while writing. Later, endeavor to hear mentally what you write. Your ultimate object is to hear without singing. Sing rhythmically all the groups you have written.

Exercise III.

Sing the following melodies from the staff, adopting the procedure given here:

(a) Tap the rhythm.

(b) Sing mentally, noting the intervals.

(c) Sing on "la." Do not stop to correct errors, but preserve the rhythm.

(d) Sing on number names or syllables as in Ex. 1.

(e) Sing on pitch (letter) names, starting on several other key-notes.

Exercise IV.

Transpose the melodies of Ex. III at the piano, thinking the intervals. This should not be difficult after the preceding keyboard drills.

Additional examples of fourths and fifths
Locate the perfect fourths and fifths in the following excerpts.

Tschaikowsky: *Sym. No. 6 Mov. 3*

Verdi: *Otello, "Brindisi" (Act I)*

Giordano: *Andrea Chenier, Duet (Act IV)*

Mahler: *Sym. No. 1*

Horns   Violins

Examples from contemporary music

Hindemith: *Piano Sonata No. 3*

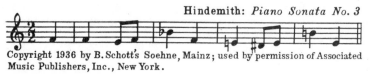

Hindemith: *Übung, Op. 37*

Samuel Barber: *Piano Sonata, Op. 26*

Roy Harris: *Piano Sonata, Scherzo*

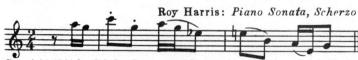

Bartok: *Three Burlesques, No. 1*

Vaughan Williams: *Sym. No. 4, Finale*

Vaughan Williams: *Sym. No. 4, Scherzo*

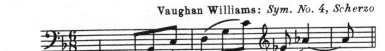

In the following, write a perfect 4th *above* each note of the upper staff and a perfect 4th *below* each note of the lower staff. Play the completed passage and locate in Gian Carlo Menotti's opera *The Medium* where Monica sings, "Mother, mother, are you there?"

Continue the following pattern based on perfect 4ths until you reach the note in the final measure. Find similar passages in Opus 32 by Ernst Toch.

etc.

In the following example, notice the descending perfect 4ths in the upper staff and the figures in the bass which include perfect 4ths.

Prokofieff: *Piano Sonata, Op. 84*

Chapter II.

Large and small thirds. Development of mode.
The remaining tones of the key.

Experiment I.

After establishing the rhythm in exercise 11(a) sing a tone to complete the last measure. Compare your result with (b).

In exercise 12 sing a tone in the second measure which will lie between 1 and 5. The tone which seems most natural to sing is the third above the tonic. Since there are three staff degrees contained in this interval, it is called a *third*.

Compare the *third* with the perfect 4th and perfect 5th of the preceding lesson. It is more pleasing to the ear and does not have the hollow quality of the perfect intervals.

Sing the third shown at (c) of Ex. 12 and compare it with the third shown at (d). Compare the intervals as to size. The first is as large as two whole steps. It is called a *large* (also called major) *third*. The second interval contains one and a half steps. It is called a *small* (also called minor) *third*.

Listening Drill.

1. Have the following examples played. Sing them from memory and discover the two types of thirds. Compare them as to quality.

Singing Drills.

1. Sing large thirds from many pitches.

2. Sing small thirds from many pitches.

3. Play the lower tone and sing the upper.

4. Play the upper tone and sing the lower.

5. In class work the class is divided in two sections and the two types of thirds are sung in parts.

Keyboard Practice.

1. Play large thirds on every key within the octave, starting on middle C. Think the size of the interval (two whole steps). Refer to Ex. 14(a).

2. Play small thirds on every key within the octave, starting on middle C. Think the size of the interval (1½ steps). Refer to Ex. 14(b).

3. Play the following sequences. Think the size of the intervals and say the letter names before playing. Practice until the playing is automatic.

Writing Drills.

1. Write large and small thirds on the staff. Start on many different pitches and use both clefs.

Note the following points:

A third is from a line to the line above and from a space to the space above. In order to determine whether the third is large or small it will be necessary to think the size of the interval by steps and half steps.

2. Write the sequences of the keyboard drill *away* from the piano.

3. In class work, one group may sing the sequence on pitch (letter) names; another group may write the sequence at the same time on the blackboard, while a student plays the exercise at the piano.

Footnote: When the same tone is represented on the staff by different pitch (letter) names, the latter are said to be "enharmonic." For example: in Ex. 14 the tones represented by C♯-E♯ are the same as D♭-F.

Examples of large (major) thirds and small (minor) thirds
in contemporary music

Analyze the following pattern and find the large (major) thirds. The interval
in the last measure sounds like a large third but is notated as a diminished fourth.

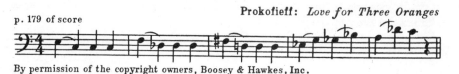

p. 179 of score

Prokofieff: *Love for Three Oranges*

By permission of the copyright owners, Boosey & Hawkes, Inc.

In the following, add a small (minor) third *below* each note of the melody
and a small third *above* the notes of the bass as indicated in the first measure.
Play the example and locate it in the second movement of Hindemith's *Third
Piano Sonata.*

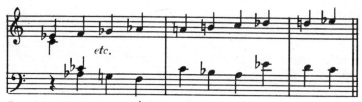

Copyright 1936 by B. Schott's Soehne, Mainz; used by permission of As-
sociated Music Publishers, Inc., New York.

Note the use of thirds in the following excerpt.

Menotti: *The Medium*

p. 83
of
score

"There is your money"

By permission of G. Schirmer,
copyright owner.

Write large and small thirds *above* the notes of the following as indicated by
the letters L and s. Find similar passages in *Omaggi*, No. 3 by the Italian composer, Malipiero.

L3   L3   s3   s3   L3   L3   s3   s3   L3

The following pattern is taken from *Riders to the Sea*, an opera by Ralph Vaughan Williams. The intervals are small thirds. Write the same pattern, starting on E flat. Check both patterns and observe that every pitch of the chromatic scale is used.

In the following, write a large third *above* each note of the upper staff. Play the completed example and locate it in the "Smugglers Chorus" from Act III of *Carmen* by Bizet.

The student is advised to examine measures 1-2 on page 41 of George Gershwin's opera, *Porgy and Bess*, which are quite similar in effect to the example from *Carmen*. Note the use of large thirds in the upper staff against a chromatic scale line in the bass.

Major and Minor Mode.

1. Sing the following tone group: 1 3 | 5 3 | 5 5̄ | 1 ||

2. Sing the same melody but substitute the *small third* for the large third. What difference in effect do you notice? The key feeling remains unchanged, but the small third changes the character of the melody and introduces a new factor which is termed *mode*. Mode means "manner." When the large third is used the melody is in the *major mode* and when the small third is employed the melody is in the *minor mode*. Unless the tempo is rapid, the minor mode is more sombre and vague than the major mode. Return to the listening drill and sing the examples, noting which are in the major mode and which in the minor mode. Compare the melodies as to quality.

3. Sing the following groups in both modes.

1 3 | 1 || 1 5 | 3 1 | 5̄ 5̄ | 1 ||
1 3 | 5 5 | 1 || 1 5 | 3 5 | 5̄ 5̄ | 1 ||
1 1 | 3 3 | 5 5̄ | 1 || 1 3 | 1 5 | 5̄ 5̄ | 1 ||
1 3 | 5 3 | 1 5̄ | 1 || 1 3 | 5 3 | 5 5 | 1 ||

4. Dictation:

   a) The teacher will sing or play the groups of Ex. 3 (above).

   b) The student will sing the melody on "la" from memory.

   c) Analyze the intervals mentally (this is merely the process of recognition and memory of the groups previously sung.)

   d) Sing with the number names.

   e) Sing slowly on the pitch (letter) names using different pitches as the tonic.

5. Write the tone groups on the staff. Employ both clefs. Follow the same procedure outlined in the first chapter. Sing the melodies you have written.

6. The technical name of the third above the tonic is *mediant*, as it lies midway between the tonic and the dominant.

Sing the following melodies.

  a) Tap the rhythm.
  b) Sing mentally, noting the intervals.
  c) Sing on "la." Do not stop to correct errors but preserve the rhythm.
  d) Sing on number names.
  e) Sing on the pitch (letter) names.
  f) Transpose the melodies at the piano, thinking the intervals.

Experiment II.

Ex. 15.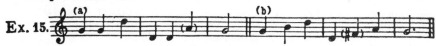

Tap the rhythm of Ex. 15 (a). When the rhythm is well established, sing thru and supply a tone on the third pulse of measure two. The tone which most naturally follows the dominant, "d," of measure two is the perfect fifth above, "a." This tone is a whole step above the tonic and its technical name is *supertonic*. Look up the meaning of the prefix "super." In singing call it 2 (two) or "re."

In Ex. 15 (b) sing a tone between 5 and 2 in the second measure. This tone (f♯) is one half step below the tonic, and its technical name is *subtonic*. What is the meaning of the prefix "sub"? Repeat the tone f♯ several times, and you will feel that it demands progression to the tonic. Because of its active quality, it is often called the *leading-tone*. In singing, call it 7 (seven) or "ti." The tendency of an active tone to *resolve* to a rest tone is called *"tonal magnetism."*

  1. Sing the following tone groups:

(a) 1 5 | 5̄ 2 | 1 ‖   (c) 1 2 | 1 ‖   (e) 1 7 2 | 1 ‖   (g) 1 3 | 2 7 | 1 ‖
(b) 1 5 | 5̱ 7 | 1 ‖   (d) 1 7 | 1 ‖   (f) 1 2 7 | 1 ‖   (h) 1 1 | 5 5̄ | 7 2 | 1 ‖

  2. Write the tone groups on the staff. Employ both clefs.

  3. After completing the written work, sing the melodies you have written. Sing on both number and letter names.

  4. Sing the following. It is an old French melody. Notice the bell effect. Write it on the staff.

$\frac{2}{4}$ 3 1 | 2 5 | 1 2 | 5̄ 3 | 1 2 5 | 1 2 5̄ | 3 1 | 2 3 | 1 2 | 5 1 | 1 5̄ | 1 1 | 1 ‖

Ex. 16.

Sing Ex. 16(a) with a very definite rhythm. In bar 3 supply the tone at ✠ which seems most natural. Compare your result with (b). This tone is four degrees above the tonic, and its technical name in relation to the key is *subdominant*. It is the same distance *below* the tonic as the dominant is *above* the tonic. Therefore it is called the subdominant (or under dominant). Refer to (c). Notice that this tone is active and resolves down by half step, following the principle of *tonal magnetism*.

Ex. 17.

Sing Ex. 17 (a) and supply a tone between the two notes of bar two. The most natural result is shown at (b). Another way of discovering the same tone is shown at (c). How far above the tonic is this tone? How far above the dominant? Since it stands midway *between* tonic and subdominant, it is called the submediant (under-mediant). See (d).

Summary.

Group all the tones discovered and arrange them within the compass of an octave.

A series of tones arranged in this order on successive degrees of the staff is called a *scale*. The structure of the scale will be discussed in a later chapter.

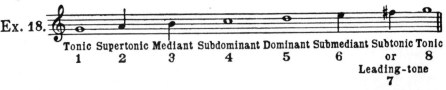

Ex. 18.

Tonic	Supertonic	Mediant	Subdominant	Dominant	Submediant	Subtonic	Tonic
1	2	3	4	5	6	or	8
						Leading-tone	
						7	

Another interesting arrangement of these tones occurs in Ex. 19. Starting with the tonic, the tones occur in a circle of perfect fifths, each tone being generated by the one preceding. The only exception is the subdominant which is a perfect 5th below the tonic. The circle of 5ths is important in the study of chord relationship, which will be discussed in detail later.

Ex. 19.

Chapter III.

Triads

Experiment I.

Ex. 20.

Sing exercise 20 (a) on "la" and on number names. Sound the notes of the first measure together as at (b). Such a combination of tones arranged in thirds, is called a *chord*. When there are three tones, as in this example the chord is called a *triad*. Analyze the intervals in this triad. A triad composed of a large third with a small third added is called a *major triad*. The first tone is the *root*, the next tone (a third above) is the *third*, and the next tone is the *fifth*. What interval occurs from root to fifth?

Sound the notes of the second measure. What is the name of the combination? Compare the triads as to sound. Compare them as to interval structure. The triads are alike in sound and structure but are built on different tones of the key. The triad which occurs on the tonic is called the *tonic triad* and that which occurs on the dominant is named the *dominant triad*.

Listening Drill.

1. Sing the first phrase of "The Star Spangled Banner." Where do you hear the tonic triad? Sing it and apply the number names.

2. Sing the first phrase of "Come Thou Almighty King." Recognize and sing the tonic triad on number names.

3. Play the Wagner motive. What chord line does it follow?

Ex. 21.

Singing Drill.

1. Sing major triads on different pitches. Think the intervals and sing on "la."

2. Sing on number names as 1 3 5.

3. Sing as 5 7 2 and "resolve" 2.

4. Play the root and 5th on the piano and sing the 3rd.

Experiment II.

Ex. 22.

Sing Ex. 22, (a) on "la" and on number names. Sound the notes of the first measure together as at (b). Compare this triad with the major triad. Which is bright and which is dark? Analyze the intervals of the new triad. A triad composed of a small third with a large third added is called a *minor triad*. The triad which occurs on the tonic in the minor mode is a tonic triad and is minor. Play the tones of the second measure together and note that this triad is the *dominant triad* and is similar to the dominant triad in the major mode.

Singing Drill.

1. Sing minor triads from various pitches. Think the intervals and sing on "la."

2. Sing on numbers as 1 3 5.

3. Play the root and 5th on the piano and sing the 3rd.

4. Play a perfect fifth and sing the third between (both large and small). Listen carefully and contrast the effect of the major and minor triads which result.

5. Play a tone on the piano, considering that it is the third of a triad. Ex. 23. Sing the root and fifth, making the triad first major and then minor. This is more difficult than the preceding drills but is valuable in training the ear.

Ex. 23.

Major   Minor

Keyboard Practice.

1. Starting on middle C, play major triads on every key within the octave. Think the intervals. Refer Ex. 24 (a).

2. Starting on middle C, play minor triads on every key within the octave. Think the intervals. Refer Ex. 24 (b).

3. Play the sequences. Observe the pattern carefully, think the intervals, and name the pitches of each measure before playing. Practice until the playing is automatic.

Ex. 24.

Writing Drills.

1. Write major and minor triads on many pitches, using both clefs.

a) Note that the notes of a triad are on three adjacent lines or on three adjacent spaces.

b) It is a good plan to write triads in two ways. First: think in thirds, as large third, f to a; small third, a to c. Second: write a perfect 5th, then fill in the third between, either large or small according to the triad desired.

2. Write the sequences of the keyboard lesson, away from the piano.

Melodies to be sung. (over)

1. (a) Tap the rhythm. (b) Sing thru mentally, noting the intervals and the number names. (c) Sing on la. Do not stop to correct errors but keep the rhythm. (d) Sing on number names. (e) Sing on pitch names.

2. Play the *tonic* and *dominant* triads as you sing each melody. Play only one chord to each measure. Experiment until you find the correct chord. The tonic will occur in the first and last measure of every melody, and in most cases the accented note of each measure will suggest the chord to employ.

3. Transpose the melodies to other keys, thinking the intervals.

Suggestions to the teacher.

1. On the first reading of the melodies by the class, play the tonic and the dominant chords in either four-part arrangement or in the style of a very simple accompaniment. Do not play the melody. The students should become accustomed to hearing harmony with a melody at a very early stage in the study of theory.

2. Divide the class in two sections. Have one section sing the *tonic* chord and the other section sing the *dominant* chord. Play the melodies and have the sections sing their chords at the proper time.

3. Have the sections sing a chord succession as follows: I--V | I--I | V--V | I ‖ Improvise a melody with two tones to a pulse or four tones to a pulse and play it while the class sings the chords. Vary the drill by singing the melody while the class hums the chord progression.

4. It is not too soon to begin the first work in the creation of melodies. Play a chord progression such as the one given. Mark the rhythm. It is very important that the feeling for rhythmic movement be well established before attempting a melody.

a) Have individuals in the class sing a melody, one tone to a pulse, while you play the chords.

b) Have the class tap two tones to a beat while you play the chords.

c) Have individuals sing a melody to this rhythm while you play the chords. Do not discuss technical features such as skips. The harmonic progression will guide the pupils in creating melodies which are usually correct.

Wait until later for the writing of original melodies, as this is merely a musical preparation for more detailed work in the future.

Unusual Employment of Major and Minor Triads.

The history of music reveals a curious evolution in the use of major and minor triads. The music of the contrapuntal composers in the sixteenth century includes triads although these tonal groups were not conceived harmonically but as the result of interweaving melodic lines. The compositions of the noted madrigal composers, Marenzio, Gesualdo and Monteverdi and several lesser known writers such as Montella and Trabacci, illustrate the most daring use of chromatic triads. These composers did not theorize about their music but were inspired to produce such effects by their interest in "color" and its relation to the texts. Following are some examples from Gesualdo, perhaps the most radical composer of this period.

Gesualdo: *"Già piansi nel dolore"*

The type of composition just discussed disappeared more or less during the Baroque and Classic periods and composers became preoccupied with the establishment of tonality by means of the primary and secondary chord relationships. In the middle of the nineteenth century, when chromaticism was again in the ascendancy, there was a reappearance of the technique of "chromatic triads," particularly in the works of Wagner and Liszt. In the following examples, note the similarity of the passage (reduced) by Trabacci and the excerpt from the "Pilgrims Chorus" from Wagner's *Tannhäuser*.

Trabacci   Wagner

Reduced

Taking the Tannhäuser excerpt as a starting point, write and play the pattern as indicated, continuing for several more measures.

etc.

In the following examples, note the use of major triads and the means by which they are connected, i.e., a root becomes a third or fifth; a third becomes a root or fifth, etc.

The following example is most unusual as it includes only major triads (with one exception marked *).

The following, which is a reduction of passages in Vincent D'Indy's *Wallenstein* (Part III) illustrates minor triads only. Transpose these patterns.

Vincent D'Indy

In the following, fill in the voices, employing triads only. The figures above the melody indicate the chord degree in that part. Play the example on the piano.

In the following, fill in the voices. The figures above the melody indicate the chord degree in that voice and the letters below indicate the type of triad—major (M) or minor (m). Play the completed example. It is from Debussy's *La démoiselle élue*.

Employ the same procedure for the following example. After filling in the voices, play the example and locate it in the score of Debussy's opera, *Pelléas et Mélisande* in the "Scene at the well" where the circles of water expand after Mélisande has dropped her ring into the fountain.

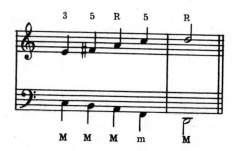

Continue the same procedure with the following example. Fill in the inner voices as indicated and play. This is a reduction of a passage in the opera *Electra* by Richard Strauss whose works illustrate novel and startling uses of triads.

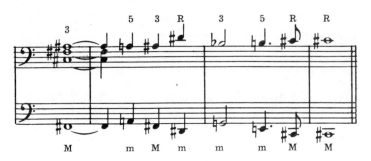

Examples in Contemporary Music.

Write major and minor triads *above* the following notes and double the root as indicated in the first chord. Locate the passage in the score (page 114) of Menotti's opera *The Medium*.

By permission of G. Schirmer, copyright owner.

Fill in the inner voices of the following example, employing the triads indicated. The large letters indicate major, and small letters minor. The passage is a reduction of a section in the March from the opera, *The Love for Three Oranges*, by Prokofieff.

By permission of the copyright owners, Boosey & Hawkes, Inc.

In the following example, write a minor triad *above* each note of the upper staff. Play the completed example and locate the passage in the score (page 43) of Menotti's opera *The Medium.*

By permission of G. Schirmer, copyright owner.

Note the use of major triads in the upper staff against the first inversions of minor triads in the lower staff. This creates a very dissonant effect.

Menotti: *The Consul*

By permission of G. Schirmer,
copyright owner.

Observe how Vaughan Williams harmonizes the "motto theme" from his *fourth symphony* in F minor with minor triads. Write minor triads *above* the notes of this theme.

Trombones
and Tuba

The theme also appears as follows, in which case the root of the triad is doubled.

Trumpets and
Trombones

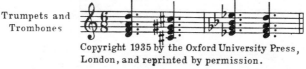

Copyright 1935 by the Oxford University Press,
London, and reprinted by permission.

The following passage can be found in Vaughan Williams' setting of *Riders to the Sea* by the Irish poet, Synge. To complete the example, consider each note of the lower staff as the fifth of a major or minor triad (indicated by the letters M and m). Add the root and third of the triad in the upper staff as shown in the first measure. In the final measure observe the effect of a major triad against a minor triad.

Another excerpt from the same opera illustrates a succession of major triads (with the exception of the one chord marked by *).

Vaughan Williams: *Riders to the Sea*

Copyright 1936 by the Oxford University Press, London, and reprinted by permission.

Roy Harris employs an interesting and impressive succession of major and minor triads near the close of his Third Symphony.

Roy Harris: *Symphony No. 3*

By permission of G. Schirmer, copyright owner.

The next example illustrates a subtle effect created by the most simple means. In the first measure observe the major triads with "added sixth" in stepwise progression. Over these chords are superimposed figures based on major triads.

Aaron Copland: *Our Town*

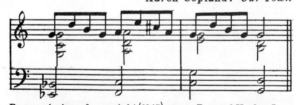

By permission of copyright (1945) owners, Boosey & Hawkes, Inc.

From the foregoing examples taken from contemporary music, it is clear that composers do not, as is often stated, concentrate entirely on dissonant combinations. They use consonant triads to a great extent, not in the context of the classic or romantic period composers, but surprisingly related to works of a more remote epoch, as described earlier in this chapter.

Chapter IV.

Scales and Key-signatures.

Ex. 25.

Sing the hymn tune "Joy to the World." Sing the motive marked (a). Sing the motive (b). Sing each motive slowly, thinking the whole and half-steps. Compare the motives. Sing the motive at (c). Here the structure is especially clear.

A group of four tones on successive degrees of the staff is called a *tetrachord*. See (d). Analyze the intervals that occur in the tetrachord and you will find that the latter consists of a large second, followed by a large second, followed by a small second. The diagram makes it clear, 1-1-½. A tetrachord built according to this pattern is named a *major tetrachord*. Do not confuse the term tetrachord with chord. The latter is a combination of three or more tones sounded together and arranged in thirds.

Sing the first four measures of the hymn tune. This arrangement of tones is called a scale. It may ascend or descend as in the example. This scale consists of two similar tetrachords.

A *major scale* consists of two *major tetrachords* as shown at (e).

Singing Drills.

1. Sing a major tetrachord on every pitch within the octave. Sing on "la." Memorize the sound so that you can sing the tetrachord either up or down from any pitch rapidly.

2. Sing tetrachords, calling the tones 1 2 3 4.

3. Sing tetrachords, calling the tones 5 6 7 8.

4. Sing tetrachords on pitch names. This will be a slower process and will involve thinking seconds.

5. Summarize in this manner: sing a tetrachord on "la"; sing it as a-b-c♯-d, then as 1 2 3 4 and as 5 6 7 8. Start on other pitches.

6. Form the entire scale in the following manner:

(a) Sing a major tetrachord.

(b) Start a whole step above the last tone of the tetrachord just sung and sing another major tetrachord.

(c) Sing the entire scale. The major scale is easy to hear and sing because it is so much a part of the student's past experience. The above process, which may seem too detailed, is done in order that the structure may be clear.

Keyboard Practice.

1. Play major tetrachords on every key within the octave, starting on middle C. Name the pitches before playing.

2. Play a major tetrachord, calling it 1 2 3 4. Take 4 as 1 and play another major tetrachord. Continue the process until you reach the same pitch-name with which you started. See (a) Ex. 26.

3. Construct the scale as follows: play a major tetrachord with the left hand; start a large second (whole step) above and play another major tetrachord with the right hand. This will make the structure clear. See (b).

4. Play the scale with one hand. Where are the half steps?

Ex. 26.

1 2 3 4 1 2 3 4   etc.

Left Hand   Right Hand

Writing Practice.

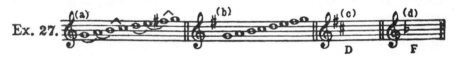

Ex. 27.

D   F

1. Sing and write a major tetrachord on G as in Ex. 27. Start a whole step above the last note and write another major tetrachord. Notice that it was necessary to use f♯ in order to have a half step between the last two notes of the upper tetrachord. To avoid writing this sharp every time it occurs, it is placed at the left end of the staff, just to the right of the clef as shown at (b). F♯ is the first sharp that appears. Construct a major scale on D, following the procedure given for the scale of G. How many sharps are in this scale? The second sharp (c♯) is placed to the right of f♯ as shown at (c).

The group of sharps or flats which appears after the clef sign is called the *key signature*. It means that you are to sharp or flat the degrees shown, and, as was stated before, it saves the labor of writing the sharps and flats each time they are required.

2. Construct major scales upon the following pitches: A, E, B, F♯, C♯.

3. Find the signature of each scale after it is written and place it to the right of the clef sign. Each new sharp as it is discovered will be placed to the right of those already found.

4. Make a table of the signatures of the following keys and compare it with the table at the end of the chapter. Keys of G, D, A, E, B, F♯, C♯.

5.·Construct the scale of F, following the same procedure as in exercise 27. You will find it necessary to use B♭ in order to have a half step between the third and fourth degrees of the lower tetrachord. Place the flat on the third line just to the right of the clef sign. This is the *signature* for the key of F. See (d) of exercise 27.

6. Construct major scales on the following pitches: B♭, E♭. A♭, D♭ G♭ and C♭.

7. Find the signature of each scale after it is written and place it to the right of the clef sign. Each new flat will be placed to the right of those already found.

8. Make a table of the signatures for the keys of F, B♭, E♭, A♭, D♭, G♭ and C♭. Compare it with the table at the end of the chapter.

Minor Scales.

Play a major tetrachord as at (a). Play it again and make the third small instead of large (b). Analyze the intervals and you will find that this tetrachord consists of a large second, followed by a small second, followed by a large second. The diagram is 1-½-1. A tetrachord built according to this pattern is called a *minor tetrachord.*

Sing minor tetrachords from various pitches. Sing first on "la" and memorize the sound. Sing on numbers, as 1 2 3 4. Sing on pitch names, which involves thinking the intervals.

In learning minor scales by tetrachord it is necessary to learn two other tetrachords. The one shown at (c) consists of a small second, followed by a large second, followed by a large second. This is called a *natural tetrachord*. Sing this type of tetrachord on "la," then on numbers as 5 6 7 8, (this tetrachord occurs only as the upper part of a scale). Sing on pitch names.

The tetrachord shown at (d) involves a new interval. Count the staff degrees. There are only two, so it is a second. Count the distance on the piano and discover that this second is a half step larger than a large second. It is called an *augmented second*. The augmented second (see e) sounds like the small third but does not appear so on the staff. The tetrachord which consists of a small second, an augmented second and a small second is called a *harmonic tetrachord*.

Sing harmonic tetrachords on different pitches.

1. Memorize the sound and sing on "la." It is helpful to connect the first two tones and the last two tones. Do not try to think the augmented second.

2. Sing on numbers, as 5 6 7 8 (this tetrachord occurs only as the upper part of a scale.)

3. Sing on pitch names. In connection with this exercise, it is a good plan to drill on augmented seconds from many pitches.

4. Sing the four different types of tetrachords from one pitch.

5. Recognize the different types of tetrachords and name them when dictated to you. These may be written from dictation. (Refer to section IV of supplement to chapter IV.)

Construction of Minor Scales.

Ex. 29.

Natural Minor   Melodic Minor   Harmonic Minor

1. Sing a minor tetrachord. Start a whole step above the last tone and sing a natural tetrachord. Repeat the process, writing as you sing. The scale which results is called a *natural minor scale*. (Also called *original* and *pure.*) It is shown at (a).

2. Sing a minor tetrachord. Start a whole step above the last tone and sing a major tetrachord. Repeat the process, writing as you sing. The scale which results is called the *melodic minor scale*.

The scale is used in this form only when ascending. The descending form is the *natural minor*. The melodic minor scale in both ascending and descending forms is shown at (b).

3. Sing a minor tetrachord. Start a whole step above the last tone and sing a *harmonic tetrachord*. Repeat the process and write as you sing. The resulting scale is called the *harmonic minor scale* (shown at c).

4. Compare the three forms of the minor scale and note the following points:

    (a) The lower tetrachord is always *minor*.

    (b) The upper tetrachord may be *natural, major* or *harmonic*.

    (c) A diagram makes this clear:

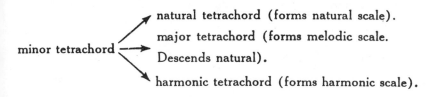

minor tetrachord

natural tetrachord (forms natural scale).

major tetrachord (forms melodic scale. Descends natural).

harmonic tetrachord (forms harmonic scale).

5. Construct the different forms of the minor scale on the following pitches: C, C#, D, Eb, E, F, F#, G, G#, A, Bb, B. Construct by tetrachords.

Signatures.

Ex. 30.

1. Build a natural minor scale as in the exercise above. Form the signature exactly as in the major scale.

2. Note the signature for the scale of C minor is the same as that for E♭ major. These two scales have the same tones, altho the tonic and dominant tones are different. Since the scales of C minor (natural form) and E♭ major have the same tones and the same signature they are said to be *relative* scales. C minor is the *relative minor* of E♭ major; E♭ major is the *relative major* of C minor. It is quite usual to say that a minor scale "borrows" its signature from the major key a small third above.

3. When a major and a minor scale are written on the same pitch they are closely related because they have the same tonic and dominant. The minor scale is then called the *tonic* or *parallel* minor. In Example 31 the major scale is shown with its *relative minor* and its *tonic minor*.

Ex. 31.

Major   Relative Minor Tonic Minor

4. When using the melodic or harmonic forms of the scale it is necessary to write in the sharps and flats which affect the 6th and 7th degrees of the scale. The signature is for the natural minor only.

5. Make a table of signatures for the minor scales you have written. Start with E minor and find the signatures in the following order: E, B, F♯, C♯, G♯. Start with D minor and find the signatures for D, G, C, F, B♭, E♭. It is possible to find the signature of D♯ and A♯ minor and of A♭ minor, but these keys are seldom used. Compare your table with the table at the end of the chapter.

Keyboard Practice.

1. Play the four types of tetrachords from one pitch. Use the following rhythms.

(a)

(b)

(c)

2. Play the three forms of the minor scale as follows:

(a) Minor tetrachord in left hand, major tetrachord in right hand. Play the natural tetrachord when descending.

(b) Minor tetrachord in left hand, natural tetrachord in right hand.

(c) Minor tetrachord in left hand, harmonic tetrachord in right hand.

3. Play the three forms of the minor scale in one hand.

4. Review of scales. Some of this work is much more advanced than the preceding drills and may be left until later.

(a) Play major and minor scales in the following rhythms:

(b) Play from any degree of a scale to the octave above and return. Ex. 32. This requires concentration and the scale must be kept clearly in mind.

Ex. 32.

(c) Choose a definite rhythmic motive and improvise a phrase of four measures within any scale. The progression must be stepwise in all cases except that a leap from 5 to 1 or 5 to 8 may be used at the close. Establish a strong rhythmic feeling and play the four measures silently on the piano keys several times before playing in the scale. Play over as extended a range as possible. This develops an automatic knowledge of the scale and is useful in developing the ability to play florid passages based on simple harmony. Refer to Ex. 33.

Example— Rhythmic motive: ♩. ♪♩ complete to 8 measures.

Ex. 33.

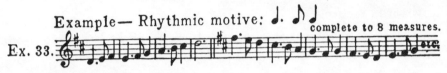

1. Sing major and minor scales to the rhythms used in (a) of No. 4 of the keyboard drills.

2. Sing the following tone groups. They involve scale passages and an occasional leap in the tonic chord.

Fix the key by singing: 1 1 |5 5̄ |1 ‖ and 1 3 |5 5 |8 |

(1) 1 2 |3̇ 2 |1 ‖

(2) 1 2 |3 4 |5 5 |1 ‖

(3) 8 5 |8 ‖

(4) 8 7 |6 5 |8 ‖

(5)   1 3 |5 5 |6 7 |8 ‖

(6)   8 7 6 |5-5 |4 3 2 |1 ‖

(7) ⁺8 7 6 |5 4   3 |5 6 7 |8 ‖

(8) 1 | 2 3 | 4 5 | 6 5 |8 ‖

(9) 1 | 3 2 | 1 3 | 5 4 | 3 5 | 8 7 | 6 5 | 6 7 | 8 ‖

Table of Key Signatures

Major Keys

Ex. 34.

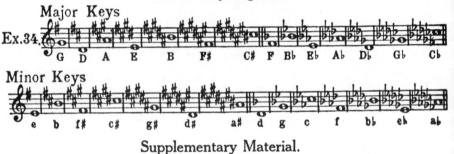

Minor Keys

Supplementary Material.

The following material is interesting and of value to the teacher and the advanced student. It may not be applicable to the average class but can be used at the discretion of the teacher.

Section I.

Ex. 35.

For practical purposes consider 1 and 5 as the fixed tones of any mode of scale. Of the remaining material within the octave there are two different pitches of sound for each degree of the staff from which to select what is known as a diatonic scale. Ex. 35. Select the perfect intervals (P4 and P5) and the large intervals (L2, L3, L6, L7). What scale results?

In the three forms of the minor scale in common use, we find that 1, 2, 4 and 5 are fixed tones. The selection of the small intervals (S3, S6, S7) in addition to these fixed tones forms the *natural minor scale*. What scale is formed by using the fixed tones and S3, S6 and L7?

Section II.

The student should experiment in forming new scales by employing only 1 and 5 as fixed tones and choosing the remaining tones of the key group as he desires. Many unusual combinations will be found. Another way of discovering new scales consists of combining the various tetrachords in any combination. Compare the results of these experiments with the table of scales which follows. Ex. 36.

Ex. 36.

     Phrygian   Dorian   Lydian   Hungarian

Section III.

Compare the four tetrachords at the piano in the following manner. First take the *major* and *minor* tetrachords. Three tones are fixed, 1, 2 and 4. The 3rd can be either large or small. Press down 1-2-4 silently, then L3 and S3 alternately (Ex. 37). Do this on various pitches.

Ex. 37.

In the *pure* and *harmonic* tetrachords, 5 and 8 are fixed. For the pure tetrachord use a S6 and S7. For the harmonic tetrachord use S6 and L7. Proceed as in Ex. 38.

Ex. 38.

Another helpful summary for the keyboard consists in the combination of upper and lower tetrachords as shown in Ex. 39. Name the kind of tetrachord in each case. Start on different pitches.

Ex. 39.

Section IV.

For a test mark the following tetrachords by scale numbers, indicating the keys in which they belong. Capital letters are used for the major keys and small letters for the minor.

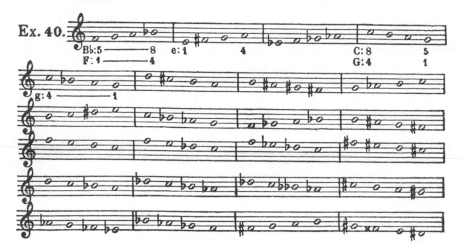

Section V.

The following examples show some of the more unusual scales.

Chapter V.

Intervals in Key Relationship.

The following work takes considerable thought and time but the results justify all of the effort necessary.

First, it trains one to think and feel melodic cadences and establish key in the most simple direct way.

Second, it provides a review of key material and scale structure.

Third, it develops an understanding and feeling for the *nature of music.*

Fourth, it teaches the relationship of harmony to accent, and of accent to accent, essentials of great importance.

Fifth, it provides a basis for part leading in the work that is to follow, not only rendering unnecessary the customary rules with their multitudinous exceptions, but it makes *tone thinking* unavoidable.

Find the large 3rds in the major scale; also in the harmonic minor scale. Ex. 42 shows a summary of the large thirds in both scales.

Ex. 42.

A large third can be placed in 3 major scales and 3 harmonic minor scales. (Ex. 43.) Follow this procedure on various pitches.

Ex. 43.

Melody construction using large thirds.

Employ large thirds in the melodic relations indicated in Ex. 43. Place a L3 in the second or third bar of a four-measure phrase, and complete the melody, being careful to establish and confirm the key.

In Ex. 44 note that the *same* L3 is used in different scale relationships. Extensive practice in this type of work requires concentration but considerable facility will result.

How many small thirds are found in the major scale? In the harmonic minor scale? Place these in key and construct melodies according to the same procedure employed in the preceding work with large 3rds.

Extensive work on perfect 4ths and 5ths need not be done. Perfect 4ths occur on every scale degree except 4, and perfect 5ths occur on every degree except 7. A perfect 5th or 4th can be placed in seven different keys (Ex. 47). Certain 4ths and 5ths are less melodic than others. Refer to all of the examples given on page 5 and observe the scale relations. Sing thru a number of melodies from various sources; find all 4ths and 5ths; note their relation in scale. "To a Wild Rose" by MacDowell contains many P4ths.

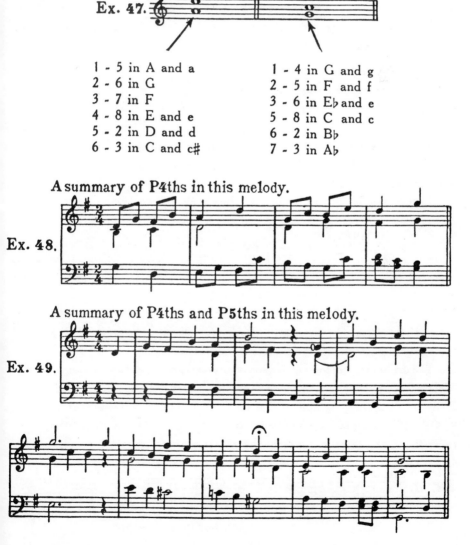

Ex. 47.

1 - 5 in A and a   1 - 4 in G and g
2 - 6 in G   2 - 5 in F and f
3 - 7 in F   3 - 6 in E♭ and e
4 - 8 in E and e   5 - 8 in C and c
5 - 2 in D and d   6 - 2 in B♭
6 - 3 in C and c♯   7 - 3 in A♭

A summary of P4ths in this melody.

Ex. 48.

A summary of P4ths and P5ths in this melody.

Ex. 49.

Chapter VI.

The Tonic and Dominant Harmonies.

The student should now be ready to leave the fundamental tone as a working basis, and work from the melodic and rhythmic basis only. Mr. Klauser made a distinction between *chord* and *harmonic* relations, the *harmonic* percept arising from a chord of definite key material. For example, G, B, D are components of a G chord that might belong to many keys. Considering the chord as 1, 3, 5 of a key, there is a quality arising from the scale degrees which is more than mere chord relation of intervals; there is a *harmonic percept*.

Play or have the following examples played. In the Beethoven excerpt, which of the first two chords is active and which is reposeful or seemingly at rest? Analyze the remaining chords in the same manner. Listening to Ex. 50 (b) name the chords as active or repose. These two contrasting chord qualities are represented by the *tonic* and *dominant* chords; the tonic being *repose*, the dominant, *active*. That the student may from the outset hear scale material in its harmonic aspect, but two harmonies are employed in the beginning, the others being introduced progressively.

Ex. 50.

The following theme by Haydn shows very clearly the structure of the tonic and dominant chords. The dominant chord includes a 4th tone which is seven staff degrees above the root. It is called a Dominant seventh Chord. This chord is employed more often than the dominant triad because the chord seventh increases the active quality.

Ex. 51.

The dominant seventh chord consists of a major triad plus a *small seventh* from the root. Such a chord can be termed a "first species" seventh, that name having reference to the *structure* of the chord and not its relation in key. See Chapter XIV for discussion of species.

All of the scale tones are included in the tonic and dominant chords as shown in Ex. 52. The tonic triad consists of repose tones, the dominant chord of active tones. According to the natural melodic law of tonal magnetism the active tones seek repose and "resolve" to tones of the tonic chord.

Ex. 52.

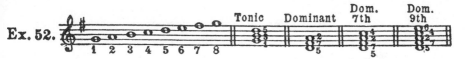

Play the dominant 7th chords of Ex. 53 and listen for the natural resolution of each chord degree. Refer to the section on triads (p. 17) for the meaning of the terms: chord degrees, root, 3rd, 5th, etc.

Ex. 53.

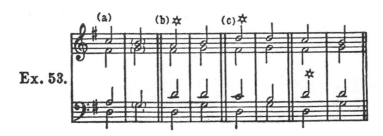

Sing each chord degree by its scale name (either syllable or number) and resolve it. Following are the natural resolutions. The bass which is chord root (scale 5 or "so") moves to tonic root (scale 1 or "do"). The tenor which is chord 5th (scale 2 or "re") moves to tonic root (scale 1 or "do"). The alto which is chord 3rd (scale 7 or "ti") moves to tonic root (scale 1 or "do"). The soprano which is chord 7th (scale 4 or "fa") moves to tonic 3rd (scale 3 or "mi").

The exceptions are shown in Ex. 53. The dominant 5th (scale 2 or "re") may resolve to tonic 3rd (scale 3 or "mi"). See (b). The dominant root (scale 5 or "so") may remain and become tonic 5th when in any voice but the bass. See (c).

The following diagram shows the chord and scale relations of I and V₇ with the resolutions.

Dominant Seventh (V₇)   Tonic (I)

Chord   Scale   Scale   Chord

7th.......... 4 ⟶   3............ 3rd
5th.......... 2 ⟶   1(or 3)..... Root (or 3rd)
3rd.......... 7 ⟶   1............ Root
Root........ 5 ⟶   1(or 5)..... Root (or 5th)

The student should master these relations before proceeding further. The following drill will help. The teacher plays various V₇ chords in many keys, using each chord degree in the soprano. The student listens to the soprano and (1) sings the scale tones (on syllables or numbers or both), (2) recites the corresponding chord degree. See Ex. 54.

Ex.54 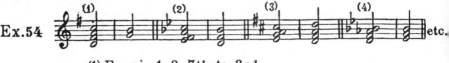 etc.

(1) Fa-mi, 4-3, 7th to 3rd.
(2) Re-do, 2-1, 5th to Root.
(3) Ti-do, 7-8, 3rd to Root.
(4) So-so, 5-5, Root to 5th or
    So-do, 5-1, Root to Root.

The dominant harmony followed by the tonic makes what is known as the *authentic cadence.* Perfect when the root of the tonic chord falls in the two outside parts with root bass in the dominant chord; imperfect when otherwise. Ex. 55.

As cadences make or mar the artistic side of a composition, their importance cannot be over-emphasized. As one should think and write phrase-wise, treating each part as an individual melody, the cadences are the objective points to which everything leads.

While hearing the parts as superposed melodies, as stated before, each tone should be heard in relation to the root of the presiding harmony. For training in this, play the patterns of Ex. 55; sing and name both the scale and chord relation of every tone. For example, taking the upper part of No. 11: Do, chord-root to Re, chord-5th to Do. Bass: Do, chord-root to Ti, chord-3rd to Do. Alto: So, chord-root, So. Tenor: Mi, chord-3rd to Fa, chord-7th, to Mi.

Sometimes there is confusion about the sevenths, so notice that the scale-7th is *not* the dominant-7th. Other relations will be employed later; the lesson now is to hear these two relations, chord and scale, so that the *nature of the material* may be the guide to all part leading.

Ex. 55.

Construction of Cadences.

Three Tone Melodic Groups.

Start with any tone of the tonic (1, 3 or 5); follow it by a tone of the dominant seventh chord and resolve the latter according to the principle of tonal magnetism. This can be done systematically:

1. Go from Do (scale 1) to Do by as many paths as possible.
2. From Do to Mi. From Mi to Do.
3. From Mi to Mi.
4. From So to Do.

Harmonization of 3-tone Melodies.

Choosing any one of the melodies, proceed as follows: See Ex. 56.

1. Choose the bass note for the tonic chords. Since the root and 3rd are the only strictly repose tones of the tonic, do not use the 5th of the tonic in the bass at present. By experimenting you will find the following to be true:

When the root is in the soprano, the third sounds best in the bass, and vice versa. It is perfectly good to have the root in both soprano and bass. Do not use the 3rd in both parts.

2. Sing and write every dominant tone which will move between the two tonic tones.

Ex. 56 .

Note the following points in Ex. 56.

The bass of (b) is smooth. The bass of (c) is possible. The bass at (d) is less good because the two voices leap in similar direction. The example (e) is entirely wrong because of the resolution of the chord 7th (*) At (f) note that both soprano and bass take the same path. This would simply repeat the melody in another octave. The idea and purpose of harmony is to add color and diversity to the parts, so the movement of the parts will *not* be identical. The movement of voices as shown at (f) is known technically as "consecutive octaves" and is avoided in vocal writing.

Before proceeding further it will be necessary to discuss the matter of *inversions*. Note that the root of the chord was not always in the bass in the melodies of Ex. 56. When the relative position of the chord degrees is changed by placing *other than the root* in the lowest part, the chord is said to be *inverted*.

Ex. 57.

When the chord-3rd is in the lowest voice, the chord is said to be in *first inversion*, which may be indicated by the figure 3 below. With the chord-5th in the lowest voice we have the *second inversion* of the chord, indicated by a 5. The principle of inversion applies also to the dominant seventh chord in which we find the *third inversion*, since the chord has four tones.

Ex. 58.

Review the work of Ex. 56, stating all inversions.

Color-Basic Principle.

Play the tonic chord omitting the 3rd. What is the effect? The root and fifth are called "basic" degrees. Add the 3rd; it is the "color" tone. In the dominant 7th chord the root and the 5th are basic; the 3rd and 7th are color tones. Experiment in the following manner: Play two parts only (bass and soprano).

1. Tonic—root and 5th; root and 3rd; 3rd and 5th.

2. Dominant 7th—root and 5th; root and 7th; root and 3rd; 3rd and 7th; 3rd and 5th; 5th and 7th.

In general it is found that a basic tone sounds best against a color tone and vice versa. This Principle will aid in the choice of inversions and should be applied in the following assignments.

In the following work the cadences are not necessarily what should be used at the close of a composition, but also what would be suitable for the close of any phrase and any tonic harmony within the phrase. This brings into use the inversions; but with only two harmonies that is a simple matter. The practice of writing and playing root basses persistently is one of the pitfalls of the beginner, and worse than time wasted, because it is a habit difficult to eradicate. As there is little good music without inversions, the habit is not only negatively bad, but positively so.

Assignment.

Write as many basses as possible to all of the 3-tone melodies previously written. When completed, mark all chords, indicating the chord by a Roman numeral corresponding to the scale degree upon which it is built (as I or V). Place an Arabic numeral corresponding to the chord degree in the bass *under* the Roman numeral (as I, V, etc.). When the chord root is in the bass no figure appears under the Roman numeral.

The following plan will clarify the procedure in harmonizing the melodies.

1. Sing melody on syllable or scale numbers.

2. Mark the I and V chords.

3. Choose the bass tones for the I chords. Apply the color-basic principle.

4. Find all possible melodic paths between the two I bass tones.

5. Choose the one which follows the color-basic principle.

6. In class work, sing in two parts. When working individually, sing one part and play the other. Play both parts.

7. Rapid drill: point to various notes, naming them in both their scale and chord relations.

Possible Progressions.

Ex. 59.

In Ex. 59 check each of the following statements with its musical illustration.

(a) The two basics in the V are good because of contrary motion.

(b) The two basics in the V are possible because of the smooth bass melody against the stationary soprano.

(c) Two basics in the I are possible, especially when it occurs at the beginning of a phrase.

(d) Altho both parts move the same distance in the same direction, this example is good because the relations are color and basic.

Ex. 60.

Ex. 60 (a). Play this example. Is the effect pleasing? Since both parts are basic and move identically, there is no contrast. This effect is known technically as *"consecutive fifths"* and is usually poor in vocal writing, especially in outer voices.

(b) Here the basic relation of soprano and bass in the second chord (V) is taken by contrary motion and is good.

(c) The basic relation of soprano and bass in the second chord is preceded and followed by a color-basic effect. This is a possible progression.

(d) In all the chords the basic relations are taken by contrary motion and the progression is possible.

Two rules are deduced from the above examples.

1. Outside parts moving in parallel motion should be color and basic, not both basic.

2. Basic relations may be taken consecutively if the parts move in contrary motion.

Write basses to the following melodies, employing the plan outlined on p. 36. They are not necessarily final cadences.

Ex. 61.

In the following consider the melody as a complete unit and end upon I with root in the bass.

Ex. 62.

Chapter VII.

Intervals in the V7 Chord and Its Inversions

4-7 in D or d   7-4 in D or d
6-2 in b minor   2-6 in b minor

In the V7 chord the interval from root to 7th (see a) is a *small seventh* (S7th). It is one whole step smaller than an octave. Write and play S7ths on various pitches. Find S7ths in the major and harmonic minor scales. Extensive drill is not necessary.

The interval from 3rd to 7th is called a *diminished fifth* (D5th) and is one half step smaller than a perfect 5th. (See b). Its inversion, the *augmented fourth* shown at (c) occurs in the 2nd inversion of a V7 chord. The augmented 4th is one half step larger than a perfect 4th.

Drills.

1. Write Dim. 5ths and Aug. 4ths on many pitches.

2. Find one Dim. 5th and one Aug. 4th in the major scale.

3. Find two Dim. 5ths and two Aug. 4ths in the harmonic minor scale.

4. Place any Aug. 4th or dim. 5th in one major key and in two minor keys. See (d) and (e) Ex. 63.

1. Play Ex. 64 and complete it. Observe the pattern carefully.

2. Play Ex. 65 (a) and continue it. Note the intervals carefully.

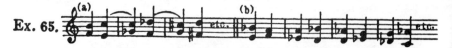

3. Ex. 65 (b) combines the Dim. 5th, L3rd, and Aug. 4th and S6th.

Triad and Interval Drills.

Before adding the inner parts to the exercises of Chapter VIII, further drill upon the inversions of triads and the new intervals found in the V7 chord is necessary. The only new intervals found in the inversion of major and minor triads are: (1) *large sixths* and (2) *small sixths*. See Ex. 66. The L6th is one whole step larger than a P5th; the S6th is one half step larger than a P5th. Notice that the upper note of a large sixth is found in the major scale formed on the lower note. The student should practice thinking, playing and writing L6ths and S6ths on many pitches. When this has become more or less automatic, proceed with the drills outlined.

Ex. 66.

Drills.

1. Find the L 6ths in the major scale. There are four. Find the L 6th in the harmonic minor scale. There are four.

2. Find the S 6ths in both the major and harmonic minor scales. There are three in each scale.

3. Place a L 6th in 4 different major scales and 4 different minor scales. See Ex. 67 (a).

4. Place a S 6th in 3 different major scales, and 3 different harmonic minor scales. See Ex. 67 (b).

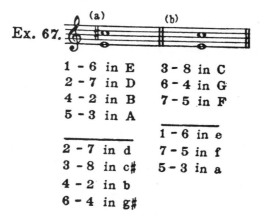

Ex. 67.

(a)	(b)
1 - 6 in E	3 - 8 in C
2 - 7 in D	6 - 4 in G
4 - 2 in B	7 - 5 in F
5 - 3 in A	
	1 - 6 in e
2 - 7 in d	7 - 5 in f
3 - 8 in c♯	5 - 3 in a
4 - 2 in b	
6 - 4 in g♯	

5. Many interesting melodies can be invented using the L 6th and S 6th in various keys. See Ex. 68. Note that the same interval is used as 5-3, 1-6, etc.

Ex. 68.

Triad Drill.

Ex. 69.

1. What is the interval structure of a major triad in first inversion? Of a minor triad in 1st inversion? Build 1st inversions rapidly by interval as (a) small 3rd plus perfect 4th, (b) large 3rd plus perfect 4th.

2. Follow the same process as in (1) with the second inversions: P 4th plus L 3rd; P 4th plus S 3rd.

3. Play a L 6th and sing the tone which will make it a major triad, then a minor triad. See (e).

4. Follow the same procedure as in (3) using a S 6th. See (f).

5. Play a P 5th in the right hand. Play the L 3rd of the triad in the left hand an octave lower. See Ex. 70 (a). Do the same with a minor triad. See (b).

Ex. 70.

6. Play a S 6th in the right hand. Add in the bass, (left hand), the tone which makes it a major chord. See Ex. 70 (c). Add a tone which will make it a minor chord. See (d).

7. Follow the procedure of No. 6 using a L 6th. See (e) and (f).

8. Wagner used an interesting harmonic plan in part of the "Pilgrims' Chorus" from Tannhauser. Note that triads only are used. What types? Analyze the example (Ex. 71) carefully, noting the chord degree in the lowest voice and any common tones. Transpose the example to various keys.

Wagner.

Ex. 71.

9. Play the following triad sequence in various keys.

Ex. 72.

Chapter VIII.

Four Part Harmonization.

Employing four parts, one tone of a triad must necessarily be doubled. By experimenting one finds the following principles to be true:

1. With the root in the bass or lowest part, double the root.

2. With the 5th in the bass, double the 5th.

When the tones of a chord are widely separated as at Ex. 73 it is said to be in "open" or "extended" position. If, in four part writing, the soprano and tenor are *within an octave*, the harmony is said to be in "close position." In open position the tenor is generally more than an octave from the soprano, and the parts are more evenly distributed.

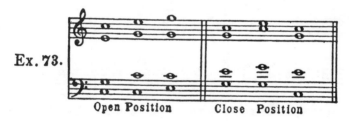

Ex. 73.

Open Position   Close Position

For vocal music the alto should not be more than an octave from either tenor or soprano. A passage may be in either close or open position, interchanging as the movement of the voices requires.

Taking different pitches as root, write and play major and minor triads, keeping the root in the bass and placing each degree of the chord in the upper part as at Ex. 74 (a) and (b). *Double the root.*

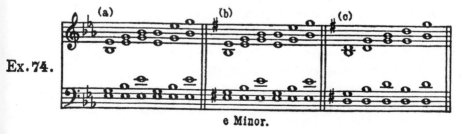

Ex. 74.

e Minor.

The lesson of the lesson is to cultivate skill in the distribution of the parts. It is a delicate and subtle art, as the different tone combinations, inversions and spacing of parts give varied harmonic effect.

Employing the chord-5th in the bass, begin in close position and write with each chord degree in the upper part as at Ex. 74 (c). *Double the 5th.*

With the chord-3rd in the bass new problems arise. The color-basic principle has already been explained. One is less likely to increase the color element, especially in major chords, altho this depends upon the scale relations. The 3rd is seldom doubled in the tonic chord (major mode). Since the small 3rd is darker than the large 3rd, it may be doubled with good effect in minor chords, altho this is rarely done when the chord is tonic or subdominant. In general, *double the soprano.*

Taking different pitches as chord-3rd, write the positions as shown in Ex. 75 (a) and (b),

Ex. 75.

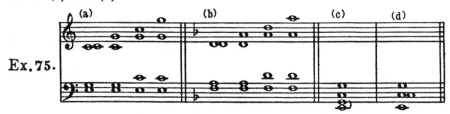

Note in (c) that the effect is too thick, so the distribution of parts at (d) is better. Pitch is an important factor. Do not place the interval of a third in a low register in vocal writing.

Assignment.

Add the inner parts (tenor and bass) to the two part work which has been completed.

It is best to have a definite plan as follows:

1. What chord degrees are present?

2. What is needed to complete the chord?

For convenience, the rules for doubling are repeated here:

(a) When the root is in the bass, double the root.

(b) When the 5th is in the bass, double the 5th.

(c) When the 3rd in the bass, double the soprano (melody tone) usually.

(d) Use all four tones of the V_7 with one exception. Omit the 5th and double the root. See Ex. 78 (b).

Ex. 76 will illustrate the assignment in detail.

Ex. 76.

I   V   I   V7   I
     7   3   5

(a) Soprano and bass given. What degrees are present in the first tonic chord? Root and 3rd. What is needed? Another root (since the chord is in root position) and the 5th.

What degrees are present in the V7 chord? 7th and 5th. What is needed to complete the chord? 3rd and root.

Allow the inner parts of the V7 to resolve naturally and the following tonic chord will have correct doubling.

(b) The completed example is shown. Go thru the entire exercise, asking yourself the questions outlined.

Problems in the Four Part Work.

1. As the root provides the basic quality for a chord, the 5th is sometimes omitted. This is often necessary when every tone of a V7 resolves strictly. See Ex. 78 (a).

2. For a closing cadence it is better to have a complete tonic chord. Because of this the 5th of the V7 (Re) is omitted and the root is doubled. Since there is an excellent balance of parts, two color tones and two basics, the V7 with omitted 5th and doubled root is good. See Ex. 78 (b).

To prove this play the various arrangements of the V7 chord in Ex. 77 and determine which are most satisfactory.

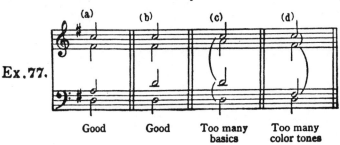

Ex. 77.

Good   Good   Too many   Too many
                        basics   color tones

Ex. 78.

no 5th

3. Since a complete tonic chord is more satisfactory for a closing cadence, the 3rd of the V (Ti) often resolves to the 5th of the I (So) rather than to I root (Do). In other words, Ti (chord-3rd) may fall back to its generator, So (chord-root). See Ex. 78 (c). The effect of a complete tonic chord is more important than the resolution of one tone in an inner part.

4. In Ex. 79 (a) note that the 7th of the V (Fa) ascends to the 5th of I (So). The natural tendency of Fa is down to Mi. Since it does not so resolve, the ear should be satisfied by hearing the tone of resolution (Mi) in another prominent part. As the bass is next to the soprano in importance, the 3rd of the I (Mi) may be taken in that part. See (b). It would naturally be approached by the 5th of V (Re). See (c). From this deduce the rule:

When Fa ascends to So, it is accompanied by Re in the bass, and Re ascends to Mi. The outer parts move in 3rds.

Ex. 79.

5. When adding the inner parts to Ex. 80 (a) note that Fa is not included in the V. Fa is a down leader and counteracts the upward tendency of Re. See (b). Also, if Fa is included as at (c), its resolution to Mi would double the 3rd of the I.

Ex. 80.

6. The 3rd of the tonic chord is sometimes doubled when the doubled 3rd is "disguised." This is usually done when the 3rd is taken by *contrary motion*, and on a *weak pulse*. In such cases the rhythm and the movement of voices both tend to counteract the unusual doubling. Ex. 81. The chord third is sometimes doubled as shown in Ex. 81 (b).

Ex. 81.

Add the tenor and alto in Ex. 82. Follow the plan outlined on p. 53. The various problems of 4 part work as discussed on p. 53 - 55 are included in Ex. 82.

Ex. 82.

Chapter IX.

Harmonization of Melodies.
The Dominant Ninth.
Creative Work.

Ex. 83.

Sing the melody above. Note the rhythmic divisions as marked. The unit next larger than a bar is termed a *section*. A section may be two or three bars, not more. The next larger group, consisting of two sections, is termed a *phrase*. Phrase refers to content and is defined by cadence, so it may be of varying lengths. The normal phrase is four bars long but we find "short phrases" of two bars, "long phrases" of eight bars, which are determined by the tempo. Phrases are also of irregular lengths as 3, 5, 6 bars, etc.

The most essential factor in the harmonization of melodies is the selection of harmonies to meet the metric and rhythmic needs. The kind of chord and its position or inversion are greatly influenced by the section and phrase *accents* and their relation to the whole melody.

In all rhythmic groups there are strong and weak elements; not only strong and weak beats in the bar, but strong and weak bars in a section, etc. The harmony must be selected to amplify these effects. The student should first recognize and mark off the rhythmic groups, find the cadences, consider their relative importance, and choose appropriate chords and inversions for these vital points before attempting details.

To demonstrate the fact that accent is a factor in selecting harmony, and that so-called "rules" of harmonization mean little, play Ex. 84 (a). Observe that while the fourth note of the melody can be harmonized by a V7 it anticipates and spoils the effect of the following section accent. The example at (b) is equally bad for the same reason. For a satisfactory result the harmony should change on the section accent as at (c).

Ex. 84.

As nearly every principle of writing can be learned in dealing with I and V7, it is better to restrict the work to the use of those two harmonies until the fundamentals are thoroly mastered. Variety of chord positions is more important than the use of many harmonies. Each position and inversion produces its own characteristic effect, and the selection of these to meet the specific rhythmic demands is an art that requires thought, experience, and good taste. The best way to cultivate good taste and judgment is to exercise it. Contrast, proportion and rhythm will always be elements of art, so when we make the study of music the study of material in relation to these things, we are dealing with vital, lasting elements.

Before harmonizing the following melody, Ex. 85, observe the following principles:

1. Unless the tempo is very rapid, the law of contrast requires the use of an inversion when two or more successive bars of the same harmony occur.

2. For a conclusive close the root of the V should precede the final I which will be in root position.

3. The quality of an accented beat or bar should not be *anticipated* on a *preceding* weak beat or bar.

Plan of procedure.

1. Sing the melody, Ex. 85. What is the tempo?

2. Mark the section accent. What chord is required here? Since this is the cadence section, what position is best?

3. What harmony occurs thruout the first section? How can variety be obtained? Refer to principle 1.

4. Which inversion should be used? Apply color-basic principle. Why would I$_5$ be a poor choice? Refer to principle 3.

5. Write the bass. Refer to the exercise.

Ex. 85.

The following principles will apply to the melodies of Ex. 86.

A.   The tonic chord with the 5th in the bass (I$_5$) possesses a progression quality and can be used where a dominant quality is desired. Do *not* use I$_5$ when a strictly tonic quality is desired. The I$_5$ can be used on a weak pulse to give variety in a bar or section where the tonic harmony presides thruout.

B.   When a tone on a weak pulse is repeated on the following accent, change the harmony.

C.   When the melody is static, the bass should move and vice versa.

Ask yourself the following questions about the melodies of Ex. 86. Write the bass from the figures indicated. Refer to the principles just given and observe how they apply to the harmonization which is suggested.

1. Where is the section accent in each melody? Is it a tonic or dominant tone? What quality is desired?

2. If the tone is a member of the tonic chord but a progression quality is desired, what chord can be used?

3. How can variety be obtained in the first section of melody No. 1?

4. Why is the harmonization of the second and third notes of melody No. 2 good?

5. Add the inner parts.

Ex. 86.

The use of I₅

The second inversion of the tonic (I) is most often used in cadence and falls on an accent. *It demands the dominant root* (V) and should be stronger than the latter. It may occur between two dominant chords as shown at Ex. 87 (a). In this case it sounds like an auxiliary chord and is unaccented.

The progression at (b) is very bad, because the V anticipates and spoils the effect of the accented I₅. Therefore, I₅ occurring on an accent cannot be preceded by V.

Ex. 87.

The use of V₅

The second inversion of the dominant (V) when falling on an accent suggests a modulation. Therefore, unless a modulation is desired, counteract the demand by including the seventh (V₇). The latter often occurs in the cadence section of a melody. See Ex. 88 (a). V^7_5 - V^7_8 is a good progression, since the bass of V₅ (Re) resolves naturally to its generator (So). V^7_3 - V^7_8 is less satisfactory. Why?

The dominant triad in second inversion (V₅) is best used as a passing chord on a weak beat, the bass moving by step. Ex. 88 (b).

Ex. 88.

Assignment.

Harmonize the melodies of Ex. 89. Have a definite plan of procedure:

1. Sing the melody on syllable and number names.

2. Find the harmonies for each bar, not each beat.

3. Select the inversions for I. Apply the color-basic principle. It is a good plan to scan the melody and name each note as color or basic.

4. Choose the bass notes for V which best lead to those chosen for I.

5. Write the complete bass.

6. Add the inner parts, watching carefully the correct resolution of V7.

Suggestions for certain of the melodies:

No. 3. The first note is called an *anacrusis*, which is the technical term applied to that part of a phrase beginning on the fractional part of a bar. In other words, a melody begins on an anacrusis unless it starts on the primary accent. Since an anacrusis throws weight or emphasis on the following accented beat, it is in good taste to leave it unharmonized, or to employ inversions. The contrast serves to bring out the accented harmony. If the first anacrusis is left unharmonized, treat the next two in similar fashion. Which of the two V accents requires a root position and why?

No. 4. When the melody begins with a long note, try a rest on the first beat and let the parts enter on the second beat. Which of the two V bars requires root position?

Nos. 5 and 6. Since the melody line is varied, try rests on both first and third beats and employ the chord on the second beat only.

No. 7. How can variety be obtained in the first section? In the 3rd bar use two different positions of the V chord. Determine the best position by the accented note of each triplet.

Ex. 89.

Melody Construction.

Note that in a four bar phrase it is possible to have the following arrangements of tonic and dominant harmony:

Ex. 90.

(1) I | I | V7 | I ‖

(2) I | V7 | V7 | I ‖

In No. 1 it is best to have an inversion in bar two. Why? In No. 2 it is best to have two different positions of the V7. Why?

Assignment.

1. Play the chord patterns of Ex. 90. Play the chords rhythmically with strong accents. Choosing any rhythmic pattern such as ♩ ♩|♩.♪|♫♫|♩‖ sing a melody while playing the chords. The harmony and rhythm will aid in creating musical melodies.

2. Write the melodies you sing. In some cases they will contain tones which do not belong to the chord. These are called "by-tones" (or non-chordal tones) and will be discussed at length in a later chapter.

Longer Melodies.

Melodies of 8 bars usually consist of at least two well defined phrases, which are termed *fore-phrase* and *after-phrase*. Refer to Ex. 83. They are also called *antecedent* and *consequent*. One is often stronger than the other, usually the after-phrase, since it confirms or completes the idea of the fore-phrase. Because of this fact the after-phrase is harmonized in a stronger manner. This is often accomplished by using a lower register.

There are three primary elements of contrast and unity: Rhythmic Setting, Melodic Line, and Harmonic Treatment. In a melody of eight bars or more, these elements must always be considered. The cadences of the section group should be less definite than those of the longer groups. If they are not so in the melody, then the harmony should produce that effect. The relative strength of the cadences must be considered. When the V harmony falls on the closing beat of the fore-phrase, it is called a "half-cadence," also a "rising cadence," as the effect is equivalent to an interrogation point. As a rule the root of V is used for such a cadence. In order to mark the pause it is better to use the V *triad*, as the 7th of the V (Fa) destroys the feeling of pause.

The section cadences can be termed "quarter-cadences." They are relatively less important than half-cadences, and *inversions* are often used at such points.

Sing thru the melodies of Ex. 91 and find the half-cadences.

Find the quarter-cadences in melodies 6, 7, 8, 9.

The following principles may be applied in several of the melodies:

A. A sequence will often require different positions of chords at cadence points than would ordinarily be used.

B. Within the phrase *inversions* are used to produce continuity as well as variety in the bass melody.

C. A long note in the melody is an invitation for movement in at least one of the other parts, especially if the long note falls at the close of a section where the cadence should not be too marked.

D. When the melody moves by leap or is decorative, the bass should be more static.

E. If the melody moves at cadence points the bass should include the long notes to mark the phrases.

In harmonizing the melodies of Ex. 91 follow a definite plan:

1. Sing the melody on neutral syllable and on scale numbers.

2. Find the cadences. Are they I or V? What is their relative importance? Choose root positions or inversions to meet the rhythmic demand.

3. Find the tonic chords in the phrases. Where are inversions needed? Apply the color-basic principle.

4. Choose the best V inversions to lead to the I tones.

5. Write the complete bass.

The following suggestions for the melodies may aid the student:

No. 1. Write two parts only. Fill in the last two chords. Refer to principles C and E. How can you make the after-phrase heavier than the fore-phrase?

No. 2. The I chord is required in the after-phrase. Use four parts.

No. 3. The repeated tones in bars 3 and 4 require a change of harmony. Which is best, I to V or V to I? When the bass is written, fill in the alto and tenor, using rests on the first beat. This is like a waltz.

No. 4. This is effective in two parts. Note that it is in the minor mode.

No. 5. Try a rest on the first beat of bars 1, 2, 5 and 7. Refer to principle D. The chord can be written in the bass staff as an accompaniment.

No. 6. Place the chords on the rests. What two positions of V are best in bar 7?

Nos. 7 and 8. Note the quarter cadences. How can variety be obtained? Refer to principle C.

No. 9. Note the sequence. Refer to principle A.

No. 10. Change the position of the chord on beat 3. Note the repetition in the melody at bars 5 and 6. This melody can be written with a waltz accompaniment.

No. 11. Two parts. At cadences four parts are good. Be sure to apply the color-basic principle to the accents of bars 2, 3, 5, 6.

No. 12. Four parts. Why should the anacrusis be harmonized? Principles C and D apply in the after-phrase.

Longer Melodies.

Dominant Ninth.

In its relation to So (the generator of the action group) La, the scale 6th, is a *ninth*. Refer to Ex. 52. What is the natural resolution of scale 6?

Employing four parts, one of the basic degrees of a V9 (root or 5th) will be omitted. If the root is present the fifth will be omitted, and *vice versa.* The root is frequently omitted in the inversions.

Spell the V9 in all major and minor keys. The ninth in the minor mode is a *small ninth.*

Instead of resolving on the root (So) the chord 9th (La) sometimes progresses to the chord 3rd (Ti). Refer to No. 9. Ex. 93. In such a case, the chord 3rd is *not* present *with* the ninth. All chord degrees above the fifth are said to be dissonant. When the *resolution* of a dissonance is a *color-tone*, the latter should not be present with the dissonance. For that reason the chord 3rd (Ti) is not heard with the chord ninth (La) in the example mentioned.

The seventh should always be present with the ninth unless the ninth chord is followed by a seventh chord on the same degree as at (a) Ex. 92.

Ex. 92.

Attention is called to the consecutive fifths between the two upper parts at (c) Ex. 92. They are not objectionable because the tonality is not obscure, and the three color elements prevent any barren effect that would be present without the seventh and ninth. In the outside parts (d) they are disagreeable.

Mark the chord degrees of the outside parts of Ex. 93. These examples should be used for ear-testing and may be transposed at the keyboard.

Ex. 93.

Harmonizing 3-6-5 (Mi-La-So) of the scale there is no question as to the choice of inversions for V_9. At (a) Ex. 94 the outside parts both leap a fourth in the same direction, but, having the relation of color and basic, the arrangement is good. At (b) the basic relation on the second pulse is taken by similar direction. It is not desirable, especially when the soprano makes a large leap against the step-wise progression in the bass.

Ex. 94.

The dominant 9th is best in root position or third inversion (V_9). The other positions, V_9^3 and V_9^5, are possible. In V_9^5 the root is omitted. When the 9th is placed in the bass it sounds decidedly like a non-chordal tone. See Ex. 95. In fact, many theorists do not recognize the dominant 9th chord but refer to such a tone combination as a dominant-7th with an embellishing tone. In any case, the *use of material in an artistic manner* is far more important than its classification.

Ex. 95.

Melodies to Harmonize.

Harmonize the following, employing scale 6th as a V₉. In No. 5 the 9th may be employed in the tenor voice.

Analysis.

Wagner used the full V₉ for the motive of the Rhein-Maidens, Ex. 97 (a). In the second excerpt (b) it will be observed that at times the chord 3rd is absent. In addition to the sustained bass, the melody exhibits its harmonic source. The occurrence of the chord 3rd on the accented beat of the second bar preserves the impression for the remainder of the bar.

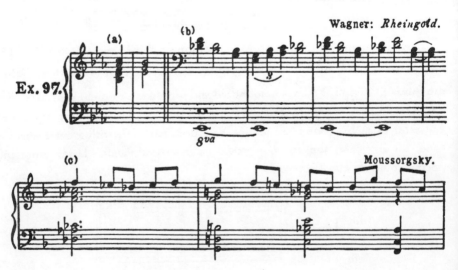

Keyboard Practice.

The following are difficult and are included for the teacher and advanced students.

Ex. 98.

The Subtonic Chord, vii° and vii₇°.

When the root of V_7 or V_9 is omitted, the resulting chord appears to have the scale seventh as root. Ex. 99.

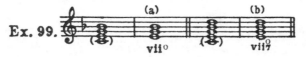

Ex. 99.

When the tones resolve according to the principle of tonal magnetism there is no doubt as to the dominant quality. For this reason the triad at (a) is called an "incomplete V_7" and the seventh chord at (b) is termed an "incomplete V_9."

Since the incomplete V7 has only one basic degree (Re), *double that* in preference to either of the color tones. The progression of Fa is more free when the root (So) is absent. Refer to Ex. 100.

Ex. 100.

vii° and vii7° are also used as independent chords. What scale degree generates the scale 7th? Refer to Ex. 19 of Chapter II. Following the principle of Ex. 19, the subtonic chord progresses to the chord built upon the scale 3rd. This harmonic progression is of no importance at this stage of study. For the present treat vii°and vii⁹₇ as dominant harmonies.

Creative Work.

Play the accompaniments of Ex. 101 and write original melodies over them. Let your ear assist in this work. If your melodies include tones which do not belong to the chord, it is correct if they sound well. At this stage it is not necessary to account for every tone. This practice is for the purpose of stimulating the creative power.

Try No. 3 as an accompaniment for No. 14 in the preceding exercises in harmonization. (Ex. 91.)

Ex. 101.

METHODS OF CHORD FIGURING

At this point it seems advisable to introduce other methods of figuring so that the student may be aware of methods employed in other texts and have the advantage of using these figures in subsequent exercises.

The system of figuring employed so far in this text indicates the chord by its type (major or minor) and its key relationship. Thus, the two harmonies studied up to this point are indicated as follows: I (major) and i (minor); V and V_7 (common to both modes). The inversions are indicated by Arabic numerals *under* the Roman numerals and correspond to *the chord degree heard in the bass.*

No Arabic numeral is required for the root position.

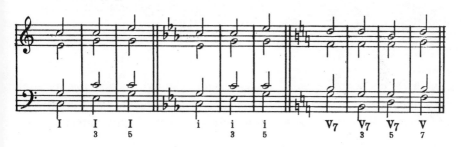

Another figuring widely employed indicates the *number* of the inversion (first, second, third) by an Arabic numeral corresponding to the *inversion* and not the chord degree in the bass.

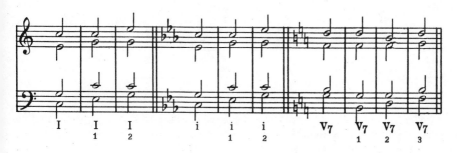

The "Figured Bass"

Another system, the most traditional and longest in existence, is called the "figured bass." The history of this system is discussed in greater detail in Chapter III of the APPENDIX. At present, it will be sufficient to explain the figuring, leaving further discussion until the student is familiar with the three primary harmonies, after which he can employ the figured bass at the discretion of the teacher.

In the following examples, the Arabic numerals under the given bass part, indicate the *intervals* to be added above, thus supplying the upper voices. The resulting chords will be recognized as those already learned and obviously the *harmonic material* is identical with the other systems of figuring.

In the inversions of the V_7 (or any seventh chord) certain Arabic numerals are somtimes omitted. Thus, the $\frac{6}{4}$ often appears as $\frac{4}{3}$, and the $\frac{6}{4}$ as $\frac{4}{2}$ or merely ^{2}. The $\frac{6}{5}$ is constant as the figures are necessary to make the chord structure clear.

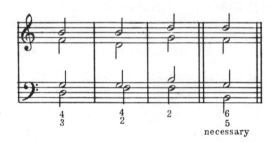

The following chart summarizes the three methods of figuring discussed. The student should employ them interchangeably, as he may be obliged to cope with various figures in different texts.

CHART

A						B						C					
Arabic numerals indicate chord degrees in bass						Arabic numerals indicate the inversion						Figured Bass Arabic numerals indicate interval above bass					
I	I 3	I 5	V	V 3	V 5	I	I 1	I 2	V	V 1	V 2	I	I 6	I 6 4	V	V 6	V 6 4
V_7	V_7 3	V_7 5	V 7			V_7	V_7 1	V_7 2	V_7 3			V_7	V 6 5	V 4 3	V 4 2		

When taking harmonic dictation and replying orally, the student should aim at being able to identify the chords as follows:

1. Tonic-three (I) or tonic-one (I) or tonic-six (I).

2. Dominant-three (V) or dominant-one (V) or dominant-six (V).

3. Dominant-seventh (V₇); dominant-seventh one (V₇) or dominant six-five (V), etc.

The author believes strongly that the chords should be named by their key relationship, i.e., *tonic, dominant* and *dominant-seventh* so that there will be no confusion in regard to the many figures. The terms, *one, two, three,* etc. should be employed for the Arabic numerals. If one says that the chord heard is a "one-three," a "one-one" or a "one-six," confusion will result. The problem becomes still more complicated if one says, "five-three" or "one-six-five."

Exercises using the various figurings

Harmonize the following employing the figuring indicated.

Harmonize the first phrase of the following melody, following principles previously discussed, then add voices above the figured bass. Figure the entire exercise.

Complete the Mozart melody using the I and V₇ only, employing the chord pattern indicated in measure one.

Mozart: *Overture, Il Seraglio*

The I and V₇ chords were introduced in an excerpt from Symphony No. 1 by Beethoven (Ex. 50 a). This symphony was composed when the composer was only thirty years old. At the close of his life when he wrote the string quartet, Op. 135, these same chords were sufficient to express some of his most inspired thoughts, as demonstrated in the following passage.

In measures five and six the V chords indicate progress to their respective tonic keys, but the effect is transitory and the tonality of D flat is clear. Fill in the inner voices according to the given bass.

From this point on there are many exercises in the text which are based on either the figuring (I I I etc.) or on the traditional figured bass. Those students
                    1 2
who wish to gain further experience and greater competency in this technique are advised to read Chapter III of the Appendix carefully and work out the figured basses given there. This experience is necessary before one can cope with the series of "compositional techniques" outlined at the close of the book.

Supplementary Material.

The following material is perhaps too difficult for the average student. It is valuable for advanced students and teachers.

The Movement of Parts.

In Ex. 56 (*f*) it was said that two parts moving in unison gave a weaker effect, because it practically made one part less. If all of the parts are taken in unison, the passage is stronger, and parts are doubled (giving the appearance of five or more) when more strength or harmonic weight is desired. In this case there are consecutive octaves, doubled thirds, etc.

Consecutive octaves are also allowed when the second chord is another position of the first:

Ex.102.

Handel: *Messiah.*

Remember that consecutive octaves, fifths and fourths, are so considered only when they occur between the *same parts.*   Consecutive unisons are considered the same as consecutive octaves.

In the previous lessons, consecutive pure fifths between outside parts were said to be undesirable. They are not unusual between middle parts, or between the two upper parts, but between the outside parts the lack of contrast is undesirable and the tonality is obscure unless the seventh is present. With a succession like Ex. 103, there is no feeling for key:

Ex. 103.

Like consecutive octaves, there is no objection to fifths when the second chord is another position of the first.

Consecutive 5ths are also considered good when moving by small 2nds or against a pedal point.

In example 3, the fifths between the bass and tenor are justified by the common tone, also by the sequence. The repetition of a seeming irregularity shows that the latter was not accidental, but intentional. Play this, following the sequence through the sharp keys back to the key of C.

The fifths between the bass and tenor of Ex. 105, No. 1, produce no disagreeable effect because the tonality is unmistakable; also because there is a common basic tone, and in the second chord the common tone becomes chord root, secondary in importance to its use in the preceding chord. The five parts of the chord falling on the accent cover the thinness that would be heard between the alto and soprano if the extra A were not there.

At No. 2 the chord-5th is taken as root on the accent, but the fifths between the outside parts are exceptional. So-called irregularities are more often found in orchestral scores.

Again and again they have been found with all of the voices moving in the same direction, and the last 5th or the close of the passage taken by leap:

A good composer employs anything that will express his ideas; but the student should first learn the natural, logical use of his music material, and not try to use for a simple text what experienced composers employ for tragic or lofty themes, subtle effects, and unusual conditions.

These examples are given, not for the student to imitate, but to show that, with all of their liberty, good composers follow certain principles, and have good reasons that a student might not understand until after much work and the analysis of the best music. The best working basis is the principle of relationship, especially to the *accent*.

The examples have also been given for the less experienced teachers who have been taught to think that the rules forbidding fifths were as binding as the ten commandments. Nearly all of the traditional rules were made for vocal music. As a matter of course they do not all apply to instrumental music. The timbre of different instruments produces effects that would be unpleasant for voices.

One should never lose sight of the relation between the metric accents of the outside parts. At Ex. 107 the impression of the first chord is not erased by the short duration of the first G in the melody and the fifths between accents. If the second note fell on the secondary accent as at No. 2, the impression of the first would be destroyed, and there would be no effect of fifths. The same principle applies to the octaves of Nos. 3 and 4.

Ex.107.

Bad   Good

a) All theorists approve of fifths when the second one is diminished, Ex. 107, No. 5. The tonal principle back of the rule is that the fifths are not basic to basic, but basic to color. The fifths between the alto and soprano of the last two chords are good because the outside parts are basic and color, and the seventh is present in the V.

b) For the approach to an accented I, the contrary direction with two color or two basic degrees is sometimes preferred: Ex. 107, Nos. 7 and 8. Remember, this color principle applies to the selection of parts for *inversions* only. If the rhythm requires the stability of root basses, they should be employed, regardless of the color principle.

In its relation to the whole, a rhythmo-melodic group may require the strength and conclusiveness of root basses. In contrast to that, there are groups that require the lighter effect of inversions. *Unless taken in contrary direction, the basic and color relation for inversions is usually better than both color or both basic.*

Keyboard Practice.

A *Sequence* is a tone figure repeated on different degrees of the scale. It may occur in harmony or in melody. There are two kinds, *Tonal* and *Real;* the former remaining in the key (a), the latter an exact reproduction necessitating a modulation for each figure (b).

Ex.108.

(a)   Scarlatti: *Pastorale.*   etc. Tonal

(b)   Beethoven: Op.10.   Real

By adding a small 7th to a major triad, converting it into a dominant 7th chord and making an enharmonic change from G♭ to F♯, a harmonic sequence of V7-I can be made through six flats and six sharps back to the key of C:

Ex. 109.

a) Another sequence of V 7-I may be effected through a common tone, the root of I being taken as 3rd of V 7 (a), also as 5th of V 7 (b):

Ex. 110.

b) Another common change is from V7 to V7. Observe the root relations:

Ex. 111.

Chapter X.

Bytones.

Play the example by Brahms (Ex. 112). Sing the melody which occurs in the inner voice of the treble staff and play the other parts. Brahms employed the tonic harmony for the entire scale. Mark all the tones which do not belong to the I. They are called *bytones* (or non-chordal tones). The best music includes a free use of bytones. The term is a *general one*, and there are *various kinds*, which will be discussed later.

Ex. 112.

They are introduced at this time because they occur in simple short melodies. One should begin to use them while the harmony is easy, and have the advantage of using them through the remainder of the work. All there is to know about them can be learned in connection with the tonic and dominant harmonies, and it is much easier than it would be later with more complex harmony.

The habit of harmonizing every note results in heavy, uninteresting work that could never be used in a good composition, so it is a *bad* habit. Even if first impressions were not lasting, it is a waste of time to do any work that could not be embodied in something larger and more important.

The early use of the embellishments or non-chordal tones is both possible and natural when one works from the melodic and rhythmic basis. Intelligent, desirable results necessitate thinking in large, rhythmo-melodic groups that must include bytones.

The melody at (a) Ex. 113 contains harmony tones only. At (b) there are bytones in the first two bars, neither of them disturbing the harmony in the least, or creating a feeling for a different harmonization, when sung at the normal tempo.

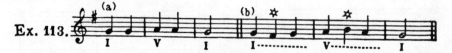

Ex. 113.

The type of bytone occurring at ✿ is called an *Auxiliary*.

Notice that it moves back to the *same* harmony tone which precedes it. One of the auxiliaries at (b) is *below* the harmony tones and one is *above* them. When it is above the harmony tone it is usually diatonic, (i.e. in the scale). When below the harmony tone it is usually a half step and may be either diatonic or chromatic.

If the auxiliary is an upleader like (a) of Ex. 114, a chromatic is unnecessary. If the auxiliary is a down-leader, a chromatic is often employed as at (b). When the auxiliary is a repose tone, as at (c), a chromatic may be used to give "direction" to the melody.

Ex. 114.

Auxiliary tones may be employed in more than one part, provided that characteristic tones of the harmony are retained in the other parts. In the Schumann example, Ex. 115, the identity of the chord is preserved by the root and third.

Ex. 115.

When an auxiliary leaps to another auxiliary on the opposite side of the harmony tone and then returns to it, the two are called *Changing Tones:* Ex. 116.

Ex. 116.

Mark the auxiliaries and changing tones in Ex. 117, indicating with a dash through the note or by the letter "a":

Ex. 117.

When a bytone moves by step to another harmony tone instead of returning to the first tone, it is called a *Passing Tone.* It may be chromatic or diatonic, and may resolve on a tone of the same harmony, or of a different harmony. See Ex. 118.

Ex. 118.

Refer back to the Brahms example (Ex. 112) and answer the following questions.

1. Which passing tones are unaccented?

2. Which passing tone occurs on a *primary accent?*

3. Which passing tone occurs on the accented part of a pulse?

The example is an excellent summary of the different types of passing tones considered from a rhythmic angle.

Summary.

1. (a) An auxiliary returns to the *same* harmony tone which precedes it.

    (b) Auxiliaries may be upper or lower, diatonic or chromatic.

2. (a) A passing tone moves to *another* tone of the same harmony or to a tone of a different harmony. Passing tones move *by step*.

    (b) Passing tones may be accented or unaccented, and diatonic or chromatic.

Melodies to Harmonize.

The following melodies contain auxiliaries and passing tones of all types. No. 4 includes an accented passing tone.

Bytones may be employed in the bass and tenor of No. 5. Try a passing tone in the bass of bar two, also an auxiliary. Try a passing tone in the tenor, second half of bar three.

Ex. 119.

Original Melodies.

Continue the practice of melody-writing as outlined in Chapter III. At this stage the student should work more intelligently, having greater experience in the harmonization of melodies, analysis, etc.

1. Plan the cadences and harmonic regulation first.

2. If it is difficult to hear a melody, play the chords and allow the harmony and rhythm to generate the melody.

3. Criticise the melody from the following outline:

    (a) Unity—a short melody should not contain too many different ideas.

    (b) Variety—avoid monotonous repetitions.

    (c) Balance—are the phrases sufficiently unified by having certain *similar* melodic and rhythmic figures?

Ex. 120 shows a chord progression and a melody generated from it.

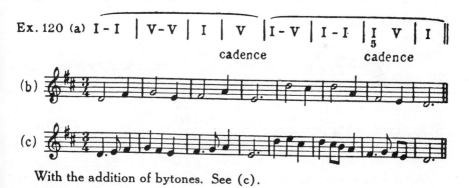

With the addition of bytones. See (c).

It is difficult to write good eight bar melodies with but two harmonies. The student is advised to concentrate upon 4 bar melodies until a new chord is introduced.

"Rules" for melody writing are of little value because composers employ anything which will express their ideas. All of the traditional rules have been disregarded in well-known melodies. *In general*, however, the following suggestions are helpful:

1. After a wide leap (larger than a 3rd) turn in the opposite direction. See (a) Ex. 121.

2. The active tones should resolve correctly unless they are used in a *scale line.* (b).

3. It is correct to move from one active tone to another if the last one resolves. See (c).

4. Wide leaps in the same direction are good when they are in a *chord line.*

Ex.121.

poor   good   poor   poor   good   good

Reference has been made to the progression of a melody after long leaps. The suggestion does not apply to the interval between two phrases, or to a long leap followed by a bytone. For example, in the following. Ex. 122 (a): D of the first measure and E in the second are both auxiliary tones, and as such the progressions are good.

Ex. 122.

After a leap which makes a cadence, especially if the latter is sustained longer than a beat, the new rhythmic group may begin with another leap in the same direction. The duration of C, also the fact that both C and the following F, are taken on accented beats, as well as belonging to different sections, changes the whole effect. See (b).

If the last note of a leap is sustained for two or more beats, the direction is then free. (c). Why? Sometimes the melody tone that would logically occur is taken in another octave. (d).

Analysis.

Both passing and auxiliary tones may fall on the accented or unaccented parts of the measure. In marking the chords for analysis, no account is taken of the bytones: that is, the letters indicating the chords are the same as though there were no bytones. Mark both the passing and auxiliary tones of the following:

Chopin: Op. 33.

Bach: *Bourree.*

etc.

Passing tones may occur in two or more parts. Passing chords are those in which all or enough of the tones to give character to the chord are bytones. There are two kinds of passing chords, those which might be considered independent chords, Ex. 124 (a), and those which would have a different resolution if they were independent. Just when the first kind should be so considered is a matter determined by the tempo. If the tempo is so fast that the harmony is not disturbed, the chord is heard as a passing chord. If the tempo is slow enough for the chord to be heard as a definite, independent chord, then it is not considered a passing chord.

Consecutive fifths are not considered objectionable between other than the outside parts when one tone of each is a bytone. They are frequently found in the works of the best composers, and one will notice that they are usually of short duration and in the unaccented places of a phrase. It has also been observed that they are more agreeable in the lower register than in the higher, where the effect is too thin.

Harmonizing melodies, first, hear the harmonic regulation that is in the melody, marking the sections as in the preceding lessons, *not* forgetting that the rhythmic accents are more important than any individual tone of the melody. Bytones occurring on the accent are much more effective than on the weak beats.

a. Observe the general character of the melody: vigorous, light, serious, etc., also the tempo. The longer one harmony presides, the faster the tempo; conversely, the slow tempo requires more changes of harmony, or of positions.

b. Write the final cadence chords first, then, with the use of bytones, each part can be of melodic interest as it is directed to the cadence. This will help to make phrase-wise thinking unavoidable.

c. In keeping with the spirit of the melody, the accompaniments can be varied by broken chords, rests and fewer parts. See Mozart, Mendelssohn and other classics for examples.

d. Rhythmic and melodic imitation or repetition of the parts is always in good taste and provides practice in one of the essentials of composition. Rests mark the rhythmic groups more definitely, also focus the attention on the remaining parts. If there are rests of *more* than one beat in the melody, at least one of the other parts should be written with more melodic interest. Rests after a climax heighten the effect.

e. The greater the melodic interest, the less necessity for variety of harmonic treatment. Since embellishments are for decorative purposes, the effect is lost if the remaining parts are not sufficiently obscure and simple to form a background for them. It is very easy to over-decorate and overload with various harmonies.

f. It is not usual to double a bytone, but should it be necessary, let one of them resolve regularly and the other in a contrary direction.

When is it necessary? When two parts move in a contrary direction to a vital rhythmic accent.

g. Notice the contrast of phrase and section in the longer melodies. The Russian songs are interesting with the two three-measure phrases balanced by one of six. The harmony of a three-measure section has the same rhythmic relation as that of a three-pulse measure, *the change occurring on the third, in preference to the second.* Apply in No. 5, Ex. 126.

Suggestions for the melodies of Ex. 126.

No. 2. Employ auxiliaries in the bass when the soprano has long notes. In bar six, try I, auxiliary tone, I.

No. 3. The after-phrase contains an accented passing tone.

No. 4. Try an "imitation" of bar three in the bass voice of bar four.

No. 5. Since the first two cadences are similar in *quality*, they should be different in *weight*. How can this be achieved? Include a seventh in the V cadence of bar three. Why?

No. 6. Since the accents of bars one and two are I, what should occur on the *section accent?* (bar three).

No. 7. The I is required on a certain accent in the after-phrase. Why?

No. 8. How long is the final section of this melody? Why? This will explain the nine bars. The diagram will aid in harmonization.

In section a, employ three parts and try a moving bass. Why? In section b, employ contrary motion and harmonize each note. Why? Unify the work by treating section c like a, and section d like b.

Melodies for Passing and Auxiliary Tones.

Chapter XI.

Bytones. (Continued)

Ex. 127.

Play Ex. 127 (a) and compare the bytones marked (☆) with those previously studied. How do they differ from auxiliaries? From passing tones?

A bytone taken by leap and resolving by step is called an *appoggiatura*. It may be unaccented as at (a), or accented as at (b). It may occur either above or below the harmony tone, and may be diatonic or chromatic. (shown at c).

Occasionally an appoggiatura does not resolve directly, but has a auxiliary tone interpolated before the resolution. (d).

Melodies to Harmonize.

The following melodies illustrate the uses of the appoggiatura as outlined above. Each melody contains at least two appoggiaturas.

First, plan the harmonic regulation. Determine whether the accented tones of each bar are chord tones or appoggiaturas. *In no case* carry the same harmony across the bar-line. Mark every appoggiatura and classify it according to Ex. 127.

Ex. 128.

Ex. 129.

Play Ex. 129. How do the bytones marked (✿) differ from the appoggiatura? This type of bytone *anticipates* a tone of the following chord. Such a bytone is called an *anticipation*. It may occur in any voice, and it may occur in two or more voices at the same time. The anticipation is unaccented and is usually shorter than the chord tone which follows.

At (a) Ex. 130, both root and 3rd are anticipated; at (b) the complete chord is anticipated:-

Ex. 130.

Occasionally a tone is anticipated in one voice and taken in another:-

Ex. 131.

When the anticipation tone is *left by leap*, it may be termed a *Free Anticipation*:-

Ex. 132.

At (a), the B♭ anticipates the 7th of the next chord. D, the last tone of the first full measure, is a free bytone, since it does not occur in the following chord. The anticipation tone is usually shorter than the tone that follows.

A bytone *left* by leap and *foreign to the following harmony* is called a
Free Tone:-

Ex. 133.

Grieg: Op. 6.   MacDowell

Analysis.

Ex. 134.

Mozart: *Sonata.*

Bach: *Bourrée.*

Bach.

Melodies Containing Anticipations and Appoggiaturas.

A very important principle should be observed when harmonizing the melodies of Ex. 135.

A tone left by a leap larger than a third should be a harmony tone, not a bytone. In other words, bytones are better *taken* by leap than *left* so. Apply this principle in melody No. 5, bars three and four. The tone which is left by leap, being a harmony tone, will suggest the correct harmonic regulation.

Suggestions:

No. 1. How is the second section of this melody extended? In bar four, employ the regular rhythm, ♩ ♩, in the bass against the syncopated rhythm of the soprano. Compare the accented and unaccented appoggiaturas in this melody.

No. 2. This can be written in four parts or with a simple waltz accompaniment.

Nos. 4 and 5. These melodies both contain syncopated rhythms. Harmonize as suggested in No. 1.

In No. 3, what type of bytone is the last note of bar three?

No. 6. A broken chord accompaniment is effective.

No. 7. First harmonize in four parts, then compare with Beethoven's treatment, Sonata, Op. 49, No. 2 (second movement).

Ex. 135.

Bohemian Air.

Folk Song.

Beethoven.

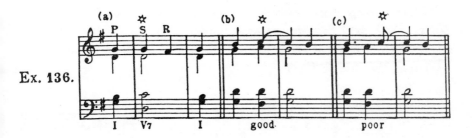

Ex. 136.

Play Ex. 136. Following the principle so often emphasized, that *when possible it is better to change the harmony on an accent,* the first full measure requires V. The accented melody tone, then, is a bytone. In what way is it similar to an appoggiatura? How different? Notice that the bytone (✴) is not approached by leap or step but is "prepared" on the preceding weak beat by a harmony tone. It is called a *suspension* and resolves down by step. It is very important to understand thoroly the harmonic formula, *Preparation, Suspension, Resolution,* which is represented by the letters P. S. R. in Ex. 136. Check these statements carefully with the musical illustration:

1. A suspension is a harmony tone in the preceding chord.

2. The preparation must be in the *same voice* as the suspension, and on a *weaker pulse.*

3. The preparation may be tied to the suspension, but it is not necessary. See (b).

4. If the preparation is tied, it is usually as long as the suspension. See (b) and (c).

5. A suspension is rarely less in length than the resolution and should be *stronger rhythmically.*

When a suspension resolves upward it is often called a *ritardation*. See Ex. 137 (a). Suspensions and ritardations often resolve "ornamentally," which means that one or more tones are interpolated before the final resolution. See Ex. 137 (c).

Ex. 137.

Suspensions and ritardations can be used together or with appoggiaturas. Refer again to Ex. 137 (b). They may occur in two or more voices and are sometimes called "double" or "triple" suspensions. The example by Bach shows a full V 7 chord suspended over the tonic.

Ex. 138.

Important principles concerning the use of suspensions.

1. When a suspension resolves on the third of a chord (especially the large third) the latter should not be included when the parts are filled in. Refer to Ex. 139 (a) and (b). Exceptions are given in the supplementary material.

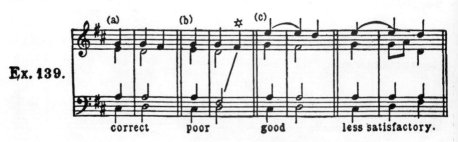

Ex. 139.

2. A suspension is more distinct if the remaining parts are static while the suspension resolves. Moving parts take the attention from the suspension and partly rob it of its effectiveness. Refer to Ex. 139 (c).

3. A tone in the bass may be carried from the weak pulse to the accented pulse (over the bar-line) when it becomes a suspension or a dissonant chord degree. In preceding work the student has not done this.

Ex. 140.

Analysis.

Ex. 141.

Melodies to Harmonize.

One of the worst faults in writing is the repetition of a chord on a strong beat, especially when the bass is the same as the preceding weak beat. The melody tone should either be treated as a suspension, or a component of another harmony. When the note is tied, if possible harmonize it with a chord that forces it to fall, as most suspensions do. By planning the harmonic regulation first, places for bytones occur that never would be found by the average student at this stage of the work.

The use of certain figures—rhythmic, melodic, and harmonic—gives organic unity to the whole and trains the student in the most important feature of composition—the development of material.

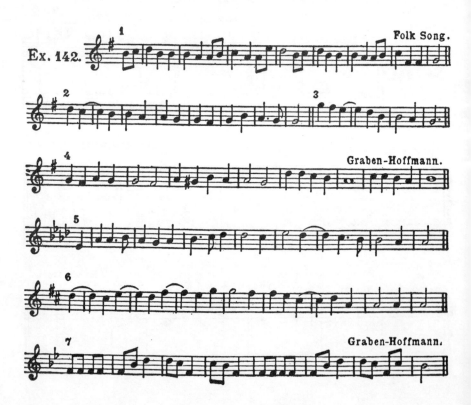

The figuring for bytones

Following are illustrations of the figured bass for suspensions and ritardations.

7 - 8   7 - 8   4 - 3   7   4- 2 - 3
              2 - 3   4 - 3

Suggestions for harmonizing the melodies of Ex. 142

A.   Try melody number 2 with the following figured basses.

6   6   6   4   9 - 8   7   6   7   4 - 3
4   5   2   6   3   4 - 3
3

B.

4   4 - 3   6   6   4 - 3   6   4   6   9 - 3
3   5   3   7

Melody number 4 can be harmonized in three voices as shown. Note the
double changing tones, the imitation of the soprano by the bass in measure six,
and observe the figuration employed.

I   vii°   V₇   I   I   I   V   vii° I V   I
          1   1   1   2

Harmonize number 7 in four voices using the following figured bass.

4   6   7   9 - 8   4   6   6-5 7
2   6 - 5   2

This melody can also be harmonized in a "free" pianistic style.

Allegretto

Added Sixth.

Another species of bytone is the *added sixth*, first introduced by Rameau. The added sixth is "La" (scale 6th) which can be sounded with the tonic chord without disturbing the harmony. The added sixth is dissonant with the chord fifth. Without the presence of the chord fifth, a tone cannot be considered an added sixth. MacDowell uses the I+6 in many of his works. "The Water Lily" is a good example.

Ex. 143.

I+6   I+6

The Pedal Point.

The *pedal point* (also called Organ Point) is a tone sustained by one part through a succession of harmonies of which it forms no part. It may be other tones of the scale, but it is oftener 1 or 5, and sometimes both.

1. A Pedal Point should enter and close as a harmony tone, and it is better entered on the accent at the beginning of a phrase. It may occur in any part, and in modern music is sometimes the only thread that holds a passage together.

2. Occurring in the bass, it produces a more tranquil effect and serves as an excellent background for an elaborate melody, or one with wide leaps. In orchestral compositions one hears the *pedal chord* against which themes are played.

3. When the pedal forms no part of the chord above it, the next tone above the pedal is regarded as the bass and the chords are marked without reference to the pedal. The latter may be indicated by the letters T. P. (tonic pedal) or D.P. (dominant pedal), followed by a line continuing as long as the pedal lasts.

Ex. 144.

Tonic Pedal. . . . .

Supplementary Material.

Earlier in the chapter, it was stated that when a suspension resolves on the chord 3rd, the latter should not be present with the dissonance. The next example (a) shows an exception to this rule because the two voices are in unison; at (b) there is an exception because of the sequence in the alto. All rules are suspended in sequences.

Ex. 145.

Sometimes, instead of resolving by step, the suspension falls to its generator or its fifth as in the following examples. At (a) the suspended fifth moves *up* to its generator.

Ex. 146.

At (b) the suspended seventh falls, not to its generator, but to the tonic root. Observe the metric weakness of the latter chord.

At (c) the suspended tonic falls a seventh to its generator. This is good, not only on account of the overtone relations, but because the nature of the tonic, "do," is what it is, giving it freedom of movement. 1, 3 and 5 of the scale possess a freedom that is not felt with the other degrees of the scale.

Analysis.

Keyboard Practice.

Describe these sequences and play them, beginning in other keys:-

The next one may be too difficult for some students at this time; if so, it may be studied later. Sequences are very helpful in acquiring facility at the key-board; what one might term "the harmonic idiom."

Chapter XII.

The Subdominant Harmony, IV and iv.

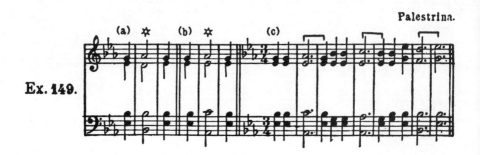

Palestrina.

Ex. 149.

Play the chord groups of Ex. 149. Note that the melody is the same in each case but that a different chord is used at ✭. The chords differ considerably in their quality but both progress to the tonic (I). The following questions will serve as a guide in distinguishing the *characteristic* quality of each chord.

1. Which is most active and demands the tonic most insistently?

2. Which is more restful and more quiet in its progression to I?

3. Which is more serious and religious in effect?

Play the Palestrina example (c) and distinguish the chords by their quality. Which is the most *decisive* of the progressions marked by brackets?

Ex. 150.

The chord under discussion is built upon the 4th degree of the scale and is called the *subdominant*. The scale numbers are 4-6-8. The figuring is IV in the major mode and iv in the minor mode. Why? See Ex. 150.

Note the common tone in IV and V₇. The 7th of V resolves to the 3rd of I as found in previous work. The root of IV, however, is free to move up or down by step or leap. When the root is doubled, one part must necessarily move by leap, or in contrary direction; otherwise consecutive octaves will result.

The tonic has been referred to as a "tone-center." In the scale we find that the lower tetrachord moves *down* to tonic, the upper tetrachord *up* to tonic. See Ex. 151. The harmonic relations are similar. The tendency of IV is *down* to I; the tendency of V is *up* to I.

Ex. 151.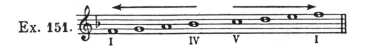

Since the IV is as far *below* I as the V is *above* I, IV can be called the subdominant (under-dominant).

As the 3rd of IV (La) is also a down-leader, the tendency is unmistakable. The 5th of IV (Do) is free to move by step or leap in any direction; however it is often held stationary. As stated before, the root of IV is free in its progression. Therefore the IV is much less restricted in its progression than V.

The cadence, IV—I, is called the "Plagal Cadence" in distinction to the "Authentic Cadence," V—I. In what type of music do we hear the plagal cadence? Refer again to Ex. 149 (c) of Palestrina and note the different effect of IV—I and V—I.

In class, all sing the tonic, and different members the various degrees
and the resolution of IV as in **Ex.** 152. If working alone, play two parts
and sing the other.

Ex. 152.

Singing Drill.

Divide the class into 3 parts. Sing the first measure in unison in
arpeggio form, followed by part singing as shown in Ex. 153. The exercises can be sung from the text or may be dictated by the teacher.

Ex. 153.

The following outline the chord scheme only. They should be sung
rhythmically as above.

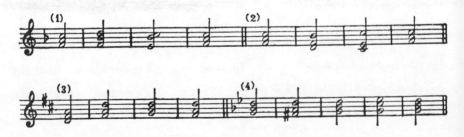

The following examples can be used in various ways.

1. Have them played for ear training.

2. Sing in four parts (class work).

3. Mark chords and inversions.

4. Observe carefully the progression of IV. Note the progression of the root (Fa).

5. Transpose the easier ones at the piano.

Ex. 154.

Melodies to Harmonize.

Before harmonizing the melodies of Ex. 155 recall these facts:

1. The IV leads to any position of I or V and V7.

2. The IV is especially useful in approaching I$_5$ at cadences.

3. Use IV or IV$_3$ but avoid IV$_5$ until the next chapter.

Suggestions for the following on pages 105-106.

Ex. 155.

Suggestions for Ex. 155.

No. 1. Try harmonizing with I and V only. The result is unsatisfactory, as IV is needed in the second bar to approach the cadence. If IV is used, the accented note of bar two becomes a bytone. What type?

No. 2. Try IV on the 3rd note. Try I₅ instead. What chord leads to I₅? Which is the best cadence?

No. 3. Apply the color-basic principle in the first two bars.

No. 5. The first accented note may be a chord tone or a bytone. Try both ways. What harmonies will be used in each case? Be sure to change the chord on the repeated notes.

No. 6. Treat the accent of bar two as a bytone.

No. 8. How can variety be obtained when accents are similar?

No. 9. The IV may be used in the fore-phrase, but it must be used in the after-phrase. Why is I₅ essential in the cadence section?

Keyboard Practice.

The following chords and inversions should be played in many keys, not only to acquire keyboard facility but to acquire a tone concept of the chord effects.

1.   I-IV-I;   i-iv-i;   I-IV-V7-I;   i-iv-V7-i;

I-IV-I₅-V7-I; i-iv-i₅-V7-i; I-IV₃-I₅-V7-I; i-iv₃-i₅-V7-i.

2. Take any major or minor triad in root position (four parts). Call it IV or iv and make the following cadence: IV- I₅ - V7 - I.

3. Memorize this sequence and play thru the flat keys back to the key of C. The tonic chord of one key is taken for the subdominant of the next, the new key being confirmed by I₅ - V7 - I.

Ex. 156.

G: IV   D: IV   etc.

Further suggestions for harmonizing the melodies of Ex. 155

It was suggested, in reference to number 8 of Ex. 155, that when the accented tones of successive measures are the same, variety can be obtained by employing different harmonies. The following harmonization will make this principle clear. Fill in the alto and tenor.

In melody number 9 of Ex. 155 which follows, add the alto and tenor voices. Note the system of figuring employed.

Graben - Hoffmann

Try the above melody with the following figured bass. Note the use of vii° at the first measure, the I with doubled third in measure three and the use of V at the middle cadence. The V is seldom employed at a cadence point but is justified because of the sequential bass.

Try the same melody with another figured bass and note the upward moving bass line and the ♯ IV₇ as it leads to V. Note also the two seventh chords in the final cadence.

Chapter XIII.

Subdominant. (Continued)

The natural progression of IV is to I. It also moves to I thru V or V7. The progression V-IV is unusual; it sounds best when inversions are used and when the outside parts move in contrary direction, as in Ex. 157 (a).

Find V-IV in Nos. 4 and 5 of Ex. 163.

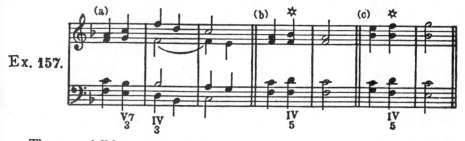

Ex. 157.

The use of IV is restricted. It is best used between two root positions of the tonic. The bass in this progression remains stationary. Ex. 157 (b). The IV may also be used as a passing chord between V7 and V7. See Ex. 157 (c). The doubling is similar to all second inversions of triads. Employ IV in melodies No. 1, 4, 9, of Ex. 167.

If the melodic line is *down* to cadence, IV will be employed unless it has already been used to such an extent that V is needed for contrast. One can almost make a rule that if the bass moves *down* to I or I IV will be employed. Try this in No. 2 of Ex. 167.

IV is rarely employed for the final chord of a cadence because it is likely to be preceded by I, and the rhythmic-harmonic effect gives the impression of a new tonic for the close. See Ex. 158.

Ex. 158.

Schumann.

etc.

Note: The bass is not from the original.

When it is necessary to employ I-IV for a cadence, the tonality should be preserved by employing decisive chords of the key, both preceding and following the cadence. Follow this principle in No. 2 and No. 6 of Ex. 167.

By adding a small seventh (Te) to the tonic chord a demand for IV is created. When the tones of the melody do not suggest IV but the rhythm demands IV, it is desirable to use I♭7. The location of ♭7 at the side of a Roman numeral indicates that the small seventh should be used in one of the inner parts. It is to be employed in the bass when the ♭7 is directly *under* the Roman figure.

Ex. 159.

Ex. 159 (a) represents the cadence section of a melody. The bar preceding I-V requires the IV. Since the melody tones do not suggest IV, the ♭7 is added to the preceding I so that a demand for IV is created. This principle can be worked out in No. 3, 4, 7 of Ex. 167. The large seventh (Ti) may also move downward, having the effect of a passing tone. See (b).

Connecting V and IV, care should be taken that the basic degrees of the outside parts are not moving in the same direction. At (b) of Ex. 160 the consecutive fourths are as objectionable as the consecutive fifths at (a).

Ex. 160.

The tones comprising the interval of an augmented second should both be in the same harmony. So when the melody progression is 7-6 (harmonic minor) it must be harmonized with V_7 and V_9. See Ex. 161.

Ex. 161.

If a seventh is added to the IV it sounds like a bytone. Whether IV7 be regarded as an independent chord or not, the seventh, which is a magnet (Mi), may resolve down or remain stationary. It may even leap, altho this is rare. In the minor mode, iv7 is an independent chord. These chords are illustrated in Nos. 8 and 9 of Ex. 163.

Subdominant Added-Sixth.

A sixth above the root may be added to the subdominant chord as in the case of the tonic added-sixth (refer to Ex. 143). The subdominant added-sixth is scale 2nd (Re). If the chord were arranged in thirds, its root might appear to be the scale 2nd (Re).

If the tone which appears to be a chord-7th resolves as a seventh naturally would, Ex. 162 (a), the chord is then considered a seventh chord, but if what appears to be the seventh remains static, the tone that moves is considered the dissonant one (b).

The added-sixth is dissonant with the chord-5th and resolves on the chord-3rd as at (b). Like the chord-7th, it increases the cadencing effect, especially with IV. Without the presence of the chord-5th a tone cannot be considered an added-6th. In his text, Rameau said that if the chord was followed by V, it should be considered a ii7. Since his time it has been employed with other harmonies with good effect. It is one of the devices that has not been overworked.

Analysis

No. 10 is an example of the "Tierce de Picardie," a major chord in the final cadence of a piece written in the minor mode. No. 11 is an interesting example of V7 to IV.

Melodies to Harmonize.

In No. 5 note that the melodic progression 7-6 (natural form of minor scale) is harmonized with the iv chord.

In composition, to use inversions skilfully is considered vastly more important and in better taste than to use many harmonies; so as each new harmony is introduced, the effect of the various inversions, positions and rhythmic relations should be thoroughly understood, heard and felt before taking another harmony. Ex. 167 provides more difficult melodies.

a. In these longer melodies, compare the cadences to see if there is sufficient contrast, also the harmony of sections for both contrast and coherence. Consider the plan of the whole, just as an artist plans according to the size of the canvas. In an eight-bar melody, mark the sections and learn what to expect in each:

165.

b. Naturally, all melodies cannot be treated in exactly the same way, but there is a general plan that the beginner should follow.

First section, establish the key.

The second section should lead to the middle cadence.

From the middle cadence the objective point is the final cadence, to which the last section is usually given.

The harmonies of the third section should not only lead to the close, but include the three things that contribute to harmonic lightness in contrast with the closing section, also the contrast of quality and quantity with the fore-phrase. The entire after-phrase should furnish quantitative and qualitative contrast with the fore-phrase. In larger forms and with a rapid tempo, the proportions would naturally be on a larger scale. The same principles apply to melody-writing. In the author's judgment, the feeling for harmonic regulation is an absolute necessity for melodies worthy of the name.

c. A vital fact to be remembered is: Where the *form* requires continuity it must be preserved by either the rhythm or the harmony. The tonic may be employed on a progression beat or bar without disturbing the rhythmic flow, but if it falls on a normal rhythmic pause, then there is a cadence. For continuity, the progression harmony should be employed at points of rhythmic pause. In other words, either the harmony or rhythm must produce the onward flow to the final objective of a phrase.

d. Look for a place for inversions in the third, fifth and sixth bars, because they mean continuity in contrast to the stability of the final cadence of either phrase. The student is again reminded that I with root bass does not produce a pause when it falls on a weak beat. Rhythmic progress is a stronger force than the harmonic quality.

e. It is in good taste to let another part imitate the rhythmic figure of the first section. For example, the first figure of No. 4 of Ex. 167.

Ex. 166.

Longer Melodies to Harmonize.

Suggestions on page 115

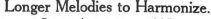

Ex. 167.

Further suggestions for harmonization of melodies in Ex. 167

Melody number 6 of Ex. 167 can harmonized in two voices with the imitative figures as shown, adding a third voice at the final cadence. Since the harmony of the middle cadence is iv, it is advisable to establish the tonality clearly by the use of i and V in the first section. Note also that since the accented tones of the second and fourth measures are the same, different chords should be used for variety. The harmonies are indicated to show that the treatment of the melody has an harmonic basis.

In the following harmonization of melody number 2 of Ex. 167 note the sequential treatment of the bass in the first phrase and the imitative figures in the second phrase. Observe the type of figuring given.

Try the above melody with the following figured bass.

In the following harmonization of number 11 from Ex. 167, note the bass in contrary motion and the manner in which a third voice is added on approach to the middle cadence. Complete the second phrase by adding a third voice (alto).

The indicated tempo of number 12 from Ex. 167 suggests a light harmonization in three voices with many rests.

Following is a suggestion for harmonizing number 3 of Ex. 168. Observe the imitative figures.

The following melodies are difficult and are included for the advanced student. Nos. 2, 4 and 5 are useful for class work in discovering the rhythmic place for IV. Four part harmonization is not necessary.

Creative Work.

Good melodies of 8 bars can be written with I, IV, V as a background. Proceed as in Chapter X (original melodies). The following rhythmic diagrams will aid in obtaining variety and will develop skill in manipulating the material.

Directions:

The small letters indicate "sections"; the capital letters indicate phrases. The exact repetition of a section is shown by 「a¬ 「a¬. The sign, "a₁," means a sequence of (a) on a different pitch. The letters b, c, d mean sections of different material. Sometimes a phrase is to be written without division into sections as at ✫.

Ex. 169.

1.
  A   B
  a a b c

4.
  A   B
  a b c d

2.
  A   B
  a a₁ b c

5.
  A   B
  a a₁ ✫

3.
  A   B
  a b b₁ c

6.
  A   B
  a b ✫

Write original melodies over the following accompaniments:

Ex. 170.

Harmonize the original melodies of Ex. 169, employing the various accompaniment figures which have been given.

Supplementary Material.

Play the following chord patterns in many keys.

In this sequence the tonic root is taken as third of a new tonic, with the small seventh in the lowest part demanding the first inversion of the subdominant chord:

The next transition is effected by means of a common tone:

Begin in different keys, and follow the same pattern in the minor mode:

Chapter XIV.

The Supertonic Harmony, ii and ii°.

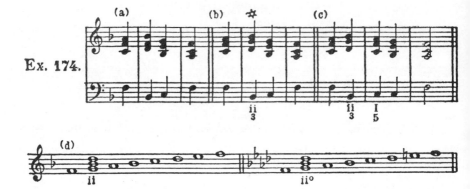

Ex. 174.

Play Ex. 174 (a) and then (b). The chords on the first accent are quite similar in effect. Compare them. What new scale degree is found in the chord at (★) in example (b)?

Constructing chords on the supertonic (scale-2nd) what type of chord is found in the major key? In the harmonic minor? Refer to (d) above. The minor supertonic is marked ii. The supertonic triad in the harmonic minor scale is a *diminished triad* and is marked ii°, the small circle indicating "diminished."

Spell minor triads on various pitches and then place in key as ii. For example: a minor triad on e is e-g-b. This is ii in the key of D major.

Spell diminished triads on various pitches and place in key as ii°. The diminished triad is composed of two small thirds. What is the interval from root to 5th? Since there has been no drill thus far on the diminished triad, this section of the drill should be very thorough.

Resolution and Progression of ii and ii°.

Referring to the circle of 5ths (Chapter II, Ex. 19) it is seen that the scale 5th (So) generates the scale 2nd (Re). As every chord resolves on its generator, ii demands V. Very frequently ii is followed by I_5, since the latter is similar in quality to V. See Ex. 174 (c).

Any chord may be followed by any other, but the natural resolution is the first thing for the student to learn and follow, after which the irregular resolutions can be practiced intelligently.

Because of bytones and the omission of the root, one cannot always analyze by arranging the tones in 3rds, but *a chord may be identified by the relations in which it appears, and by what it demands.* It may not progress to what it demands but the *demand* is one of the characteristics by which it may be known.

ii to I is sometimes found in serious, religious music, as will be seen in the analysis.

The ii is often called a "substitutional" harmony. Being closely related to the IV it is the substitute for that chord. In general, a substitutional chord does not progress to its principal chord. Therefore, ii to IV is seldom found. Usually a chord will progress to a *more active* chord. Since ii contains three active scale tones, it tends to move to V or V7 rather than to IV. Exceptions to this principle are given later.

In the first melodies for harmonization, allow ii to progress only to V or I, or to another position of itself.
5

Doubling.

The minor triads of a key (ii, iii, vi) are termed *"secondary"* chords in distinction to the *"primary"* chords (I, IV, V). The 3rd of each secondary triad is a *primary tone.* Therefore, it is good to double the 3rd of a secondary triad as it strengthens the key feeling or tonality.

Notice that in Ex. 174 the first inversion of the supertonic (ii) was used. This is employed more often than the root position. What scale degree occurs in the bass in ii? When this degree is doubled it emphasises the subdominant quality and leads strongly to cadence. It is possible to double the root of ii, especially in the root position. Unlike the primary harmonies, the chord-5th is seldom omitted. When the 5th is omitted it is difficult to tell whether the chord is major or minor.

In the *minor* mode the supertonic is almost always used in *first inversion* (ii°) and the *third doubled.* One is less likely to double the root or fifth of a diminished triad since they are dissonant degrees. Double the *third,* since it is consonant with *both* root and fifth.

Harmonization of Melodies.

Before harmonizing the following melodies, analyze the first five examples of the section marked "Analysis." In these simpler melodies follow the principles for doubling and resolution given in preceding paragraphs.

The Supertonic Seventh.

The supertonic seventh chord consists of the triad plus a seventh from the root. What scale degree is the 7th of ii? The structure of a ii$_7$ is a minor triad plus a small seventh. The chord may be termed a *second species chord*. The ii°$_7$ in the minor mode is a *third species chord*. Compare the ii$_7$ and ii°$_7$ with the V$_7$ in regard to structure.

The resolution of ii$_7$ and ii°$_7$ is to V, V$_7$, or I, as in the case of the triad. Secondary seventh chords are used more freely today than when the old harmony texts were written. The many rules concerning resolution are now superfluous. Since the 7th of ii is the tonic, "Do," it is quite free to remain stationary or leap. See No. 11 of the Analysis. The *natural tendency* for a chord seventh is to resolve down. This is particularly true when the 7th is heard *in the bass*. It is best for at least two voices to resolve regularly. Refer to Ex. 177.

Ex. 177

On different notes write and resolve the two species of supertonic 7th chords in the four positions.

Ex. 178.

More Unusual Progressions of the Supertonic.

1. The supertonic is frequently altered to a major chord by sharping the 3rd. What scale degree is this? If a chord chromatically altered is preceded and followed by a diatonic chord of the key, no modulation takes place.

The following excerpt from Schumann shows a small 7th with the I, and an augmented 4th of the scale used as 3rd of the supertonic, altering the latter to a major chord. Neither of these chromatic alterations effects a modulation, because they are not followed by a cadence or chords that confirm the suggested change of key.

Mark the major supertonic (marked II) and notice the resolution of the chord-3rd (#4 of scale). It may resolve up or down by half step. For examples of II and II₇ see Nos. 11, 12, 13, 15 of the Analysis.

Ex. 179.

Schumann.

2. Refer again to the circle of 5ths. ii is in the direct line of progress to I. If a direct movement to cadence is desired, ii-V-I is better than moving from ii to IV on the opposite side of the tone center and then back to V. To delay the cadence this may be done as in Ex. 180. ii-I gives the effect of an imperfect plagal cadence. Good composers sometimes employ the ii preceding IV but the progression is less desirable and should be avoided until one is further advanced and more accustomed to exceptional progressions.

Ex. 180.

Mendelssohn: Op. 120.

3. Second inversion of ii. The second inversion of ii, like all second inversions of major and minor triads, suggests a modulation when used on an accented pulse. On weak beats ii is useful as a *passing chord* (the bass moving by step). See Ex. 181. The supertonic-7th in second inversion (ii$_5^7$) is not restricted.

Ex. 181.

4. As may be seen in the following examples, consecutive 5ths are not unknown, but observe the great skill with which they are written. Unless a student can do as well, it would be better to avoid them.

Ex. 182.

Spohr.   2.   Bach.

etc.

5. The following example shows ii following V. Since ii begins a *new* phrase after a semi-cadence, one does not hear the progression as V-ii.

Ex. 183.

Analysis.

Mark the chords and their inversions in the following excerpts. Observe the approach to and resolution of the supertonic chords. Note the doubling. The excerpts will give an excellent review of bytones.

Keyboard Practice.

Three and four chord cadences may be played by substituting ii for IV. Play them rhythmically always.

$$I\text{-}\underset{3}{\overset{3}{ii}}\text{-}V\text{-}I. \quad I\text{-}\underset{3}{ii}\text{-}V_7\text{-}I. \quad \underset{3}{\overset{5}{i}}\text{-}\underset{3}{ii}\text{-}V_7\text{-}I. \quad \underset{3}{\overset{5}{i}}\text{-}\underset{3}{ii^o}\text{-}V_7\text{-}i. \quad i\text{-}\underset{3}{\overset{3}{ii^o}}\text{-}\underset{5}{i}\text{-}V_7\text{-}i. \quad i\text{-}iv\text{-}\underset{3}{ii^o}\text{-}V_7\text{-}i.$$

$$I\text{-}IV\text{-}ii\text{-}V_7\text{-}I. \quad i\text{-}\underset{5\ 7\ 5}{\overset{8}{ii^o}}\text{-}i\text{-}V_7\text{-}i. \quad I\text{-}\underset{3\ 7\ 3}{ii}\text{-}V\text{-}I\text{-}II_7\text{-}V_7\text{-}I. \quad i\text{-}ii^o\text{-}\underset{3}{\overset{3}{i}}\text{-}iv\text{-}\underset{5}{i}\text{-}V\text{-}i.$$

In the sequences of Ex. 185 at (a), II is taken for V, and resolved. At (b) I is changed to the minor mode, taken as a new ii and resolved. At (c) the transition is made through the common tone and is the same as Ex. 172, with IV_7 replaced by ii_7. Play them without notes in both modes:-

Melodies to Harmonize.

Proceed as in the former chapters. First, decide the tempo and general character. Select the phrase cadences and find the rhythmic groups. Look for the supertonic harmony leading to cadence and to V. The place for ii is determined by the rhythmic demands. For example: In melody No. 1 the notes marked (a) can be harmonized with V. At (b) where the same notes appear, the rhythm demands ii, leading to the cadence. In both cases the accented pulse is a bytone, which proves again that it is entirely unmusical to harmonize in "note to note" manner. No. 14 has exactly the same problem as No. 1.

In several melodies the supertonic is required at places where the melody tone suggests another harmony. In such cases the melody tone is a bytone of some type. See Nos. 4, 10, 12.

In No. 4 observe the melodic sequence and employ a harmonic sequence.

In No. 7 notice the number of repetitions of the scale 2nd which is a component of both V and ii°. Where should ii° be used? Where may V be used? See suggested harmonization on page 131.

The major supertonic (II or II7) may be used approaching the semi-cadence in No. 2.

The II7 is possible *between* two positions of V. Try this in bars 7-8 of No. 9. Also in bar four of No. 18.

Employ a waltz accompaniment for No. 16.

In No. 19 it is possible to "imitate" the first seven notes of the melody in the bass. Begin on the third beat of the first bar.

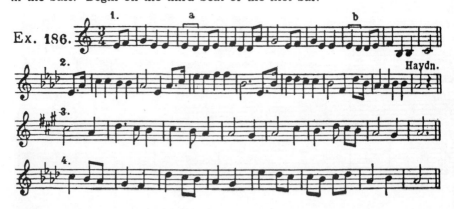

Ex. 186.

Creative Work.

After every new chord introduced original melodies should be written and harmonized. Broken chord accompaniments may be written, patterns of which may be found in various songs, Mendelssohn's Songs Without Words, the easier works of Beethoven and others. One should have a knowledge of Form before undertaking large or pretentious things. The Bach Suites, Minuets, and Schumann Op. 68, 15, and 125 are good patterns for small forms.

Analyze the form of some of the longer melodies of this chapter and use them as models for original work. Nos. 5, 9, 15 and 16 are good examples.

Suggestions for harmonizing melodies of Ex. 186

Harmonize melody number 3 with the type of accompaniment suggested for the first phrase as follows:

In number 7 of Ex. 186 note the imitation of the octave leap and the imitation of the figure in the melody by the tenor in measures 3-4. Refer back to the discussion on page 128 of how to harmonize the same tones with different harmonies, in this case the use of V *or* ii° for the second degree of the scale.

Try number 11 of Ex. 186 with both of the following figured basses. In the (B) version *double* the *root* in the $^6_4$ chord at * since it is employed as a "passing chord" and not in the usual cadential manner where the *fifth* is doubled.

Although number 15 can easily be harmonized in traditional four voice style, try an imitation of the first figure as indicated in the following.

It was previously suggested that number 16 of Ex. 186 be harmonized with a waltz accompaniment. It can also be done in a "free style" as indicated in the following.

Chapter XV.

The Submediant Harmony, vi and VI.

Handel: *"Messiah."*

A man   of sor-rows   and ac-quaint-ed with grief

Ex. 187.

Play Ex. 187. What is the quality of the chord marked (☆)? It is particularly appropriate at this point because of the text. The chord is built upon the scale 6th (6-8-3, or La-Do-Mi) and is called the *submediant*. It is a minor triad (vi) in the major keys and a major triad (VI) in minor keys. (harmonic form).

1. Spell minor triads on various pitches and place each as vi. For example: d-f-a is a minor triad and is vi in the key of F major.

2. Spell major triads and place as VI in minoi keys.

Progression of vi and VI.

Refer to the circle of 5ths in Chapter II, Ex. 19. What tone generates the scale 6th? The submediant, therefore, resolves naturally to its generator, the supertonic, but progresses to the subdominant equally well.

In contrast to the supertonic the submedient leads *from* cadence. None of the substitutional harmonies *demand* the tonic.

Play the following progressions and observe that vi leads satisfactorily to any chord except I root.

vi-ii;   vi-IV;   vi-V;   vi-I₃   vi-I₅

Since vi is a substitute for I, it is nearly as free in its progression as the latter.

Refer again to Ex. 187. To have employed a tonic chord after the dominant in the second measure would have made a perfect cadence and close before it was desired; vi was used to avoid this. Such a cadence (V-vi) is called a "deceptive cadence."

Doubling.

What scale degree is the 3rd of vi? Because it is a primary tone it is doubled with good effect. Altho VI in the minor mode is a major triad, its third is often doubled for the reason just given. When the submediant follows the dominant (especially in the minor mode) it is often necessary to double the third to avoid a poor melodic progression in the tenor or alto. See Ex. 188. When the voice leading is smooth, however, the root is sometimes doubled.

Ex. 188.

Use of vi.
3

The first inversion of vi is seldom used except in sequences and for variety in a measure of submediant harmony. It is a weak chord and quite unsatisfactory when employed on accented beats.

Use of vi.
5

As with other second inversions of triads, vi is used as a passing chord, the bass moving by step.

Ex. 189.

Employing vi or VI (minor mode) in the harmonization of melodies, use it as a substitute for I and for the sake of variety, also to delay the cadence when the rhythm demands progress and not a close. It is sometimes helpful to work from a cadence backwards. For example: at No. 11 the last two pulses will be V-I; ii may precede V, and vi may lead to ii; so the last three measures may be I-vi-ii-V-I.

Melodies to Harmonize.

Ex. 190.

The Submediant Seventh (vi7)

The vi7 is found less often than ii7. Since the 7th of the submediant is scale 5th (So), it cannot progress as freely as the seventh of the supertonic. In the progression, vi7 to ii7, the seventh of the former usually resolves down. Notice the progression of the seventh at (b) and (c). Consecutive fifths sometimes occur between primary and substitute chords (c),

Ex. 191.

The vi and vi7 are sometimes altered to major chords by sharping the chord-3rd. What scale degree is this? What is its natural resolution? When the submediant is so altered it progresses to the supertonic. When VI or VI7 is preceded and followed by diatonic chords of the key a modulation is not effected. The VI7 may, however, be employed as a new V7 and a modulation made to the key a large second above. Employing VI, do *not* double the 3rd, since it is a chromatic tone.

Ex. 192.

VI7

Analysis.

Before marking the analysis, play the excerpts and see how many of the chords can be recognized by ear. Note the movement when V and vi occur consecutively. When two chords occur on consecutive degrees, it is better for the outside voices to move in contrary direction.

One has only to study the principal themes of "Parsifal" to realize what a quiet rhythm coupled with vi, ii and IV can effect.

The VI of the minor mode is sometimes "borrowed" for use in the major mode. See No. 4 and No. 12.

When V moves to vi the root of the former is often sharped (chromatically raised). See No. 1.

The opening harmonic progression in the Prelude to "Lohengrin" is I-vi-I. This progression is rare but effective in the composition mentioned.

Ex. 193.

Taking the submediant chord in a minor key for a new tonic in the major is a very common means of modulating:

Keyboard Practice.

1. Play the following chord groups in four part harmony:

(1) I vi ii V7 I.

(2) I vi IV ii7 I V7 I.
             3 5

(3) I vi I IV I V7 I.
           3   5

(4) I V7 vi---complete the cadence.

(5) I V7 vi VI ii V7 I.
            7   3 -

2. Try all of the above progressions except (5) in the minor mode.

3. Arrange the above progressions in the forms of accompaniment given in preceding chapters. Sing and write melodies over the accompaniments.

4. Sequence to be played. Ex. 195.

Longer Melodies to Harmonize.

The following suggestions may aid the student in employing vi effectively.

(1) vi can be used directly after I as a substitute in Nos. 1, 2, 3, 6.

(2) vi can be used to avoid a perfect cadence on accented pulses in Nos. 5, 8.

(3) vi can be used in No. 9 (measure 9). Notice the irregular phrases of this melody.

(4) VI (submediant with ♯3rd) is effective in Nos. 7, 11, and possible in No. 12 (measure 10).

Analyze the form of the melodies carefully, noting the kind of cadences and their relative importance. Repetitions of melodic figures sometimes require variety of harmonization; at other times phrases may be harmonized alike for the sake of unity. For example: measures 6 and 7 of No. 8 will be monotonous with no variety of harmonic treatment. This does not mean different chords, necessarily, but a change in register or number of parts. In No. 10, however, the first and third phrases can be harmonized identically to preserve the form-scheme, which is A B A B'.

Look for bytones in melodies of rapid tempo. Employ bytones in the various parts to add melodic interest.

Do not drop or add voices aimlessly, but allow such changes to *coincide with the rhythmic divisions.*

Melodies 13, 14, and 15 are excellent for free harmonization at the piano. Further suggestions for harmonization on pages 142-144.

Ex. 196.

Schumann.

Gluck: *Orpheus.*

Further suggestions for harmonization of melodies in Ex. 196

In number 5 (Beethoven) of Ex. 196 the final descending scale passage can be harmonized in four different ways shown. In (A) one chord to every four eighths is employed at an allegretto tempo. In (B) at a slightly slower tempo it is advisable to use one chord to each beat; note the imitation of the melody by the tenor voice. In (C) at a rapid tempo the passage is harmonized with thirds. In (D) the bass proceeds in contrary motion and voices are added at the final cadence.

In number 6 the long tones require other moving parts and the second measure should be V rather than IV in order to establish the tonality.

In number 8 (Schumann) the rests in the melody should be filled in with another voice. In the (A) version there is a limited amount of "imitation" while in version (B) the imitative passages are quite extended and exact.

A.

Schumann

B.

In the following, harmonize the melody, then add the upper voices over the figured bass. Try to achieve unity throughout the entire exercise.

Adopt the reverse process with the following figured bass and melody.

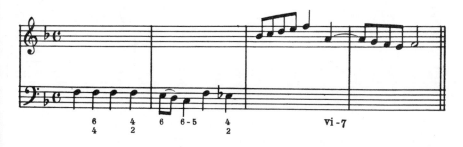

In the following example, harmonize the melodic sections indicated and add voices over the figured bass, employing full chords as shown in the first measure. In the sixth measure the chord indicated is a major triad on the mediant (III). This chord is discussed in the following chapter but can be employed now. Note that the major submediant (VI) is used several times.

When the exercise is completed, compare with the original score where the composer, in the *Finale*, derives this chorale type theme from the main theme of the first movement.

Saint-Säens *Sym. in C minor*

Chapter XVI.

The Mediant Harmony, iii and III+.

Play the two harmonizations of the scale passage, 8-7-6-5, shown in Ex. 197. In the second harmonization at (b), the chord marked by the asterisk is especially effective. This chord, the *mediant*, is built upon the scale 3rd (3-5-7 or Mi-So-Ti). It is *minor* (iii) in major keys and *augmented* (III+) in minor keys. Refer to (c). The augmented triad is composed of two large thirds. The interval from root to 5th is an *augmented 5th* which is one half step larger than a perfect 5th (d). Its inversion, the *diminished fourth*, is one half step smaller than a P.4th and sounds like a L3. The Dim. 4th is found from 7 to 3 in the harmonic minor scale.

Ex. 197.

1. Spell minor triads on various pitches and place them as iii. For example: d-f-a is a minor triad and is iii in the key of B♭ major.

2. Spell augmented triads on many pitches. Think *two large thirds*. Also spell the interval of an Aug. 5th and a Dim. 4th. Spell III+ in minor keys.

Progression of iii.

Refer to the circle of 5ths in Chapter II, Ex. 19. Since the scale 3rd is generated by the scale 6th, the mediant resolves naturally to the submediant, but progresses to the subdominant equally well.

The mediant is a substitute for the dominant. Therefore, iii to V or V7 is possible. Refer to the section on keyboard practice for other progressions.

Doubling.

What scale degree is the 3rd of the mediant? Since this is a primary tone it may be doubled with good effect. In the root position of iii, however, the root is frequently doubled.

Inversions.

The first inversion of the mediant (iii) sounds like a dominant with a bytone. The chord-3rd is usually doubled to increase the dominant quality.

The second inversion of the mediant (iii) is almost never used, and then as a *passing chord only*.

The mediant is often altered to a major triad by chromatically sharping the 3rd. What scale degree is this? What is its natural tendency? The dominant harmony is the brightest in key. When the mediant is substituted, the major chord is often employed to retain the brightness. When harmonizing an ascending scale passage, 6-7-8, the major mediant (III) is effective. Why? In a descending passage, 8-7-6, the diatonic form (iii) is more often employed. Apply these principles to Nos. 1 and 2 of the melodies for harmonization. In Nos. 3 and 4 employ the mediant in several places.

Melodies to Harmonize.

The major mediant (III) may become the dominant of the relative minor key:

In older compositions the mediant was sparingly used, especially the augmented form. It is more useful to the modern composer who expresses himself by means of peculiar dissonances and the complex harmonies that reflect the spirit of the times.

Ex. 200 shows a chord on the small mediant (♭3) in a major key.

Ex. 201 shows the mediant chord between two dominants.

The major mediant is very satisfactory for one of the middle cadences in melodies of eight or more measures. It is employed in place of the tonic or the dominant. Apply this in Nos. 2, 3, 4, 12, 15 of Ex. 204. When III is employed for a cadence it is frequently preceded by ii, ii₇ or vii₇. Why is the latter a good chord to precede iii or III? Refer to Ex. 19 of Chapter II, also Chapter IX, the subtonic chord.

Keyboard Practice.

1. Play chord groups with the mediant both preceded and followed by each chord of the preceding lessons.

For Example:

$$\text{I-vii}^0_3\text{-iii-vi-IV-V}_7\text{-I} \qquad \text{I-vi-iii-IV-II}_7\text{-V}_7\text{-I}$$

$$\text{I-ii}_3\text{-iii etc.} \qquad \text{I-III+-VI-ii}^0_3 \text{ etc.}$$

$$\text{I-III-vi-ii}_3 \text{ etc.} \qquad \text{I-iii-V}_5^7 \text{ etc.}$$

2. Arrange some of the chord groups in the accompaniment forms previously given. Sing and write melodies over the accompaniments.

3. Continue this sequence in other keys:

Ex. 202.

C: iii   Ab: iii   E: iii

Analysis.

When playing the excerpts for analysis, note first how many of the chords can be recognized by ear, then confirm by the notation. Notice especially how the mediant chord is approached and left.

Beethoven: Op. 10.

Ex. 203.

D.P. . . . .

Beethoven: Op. 79.

Bach: *Fugue.*

Bach.

☆ MacDowell: Op. 51.

☆ *Used by permission of Arthur Schmidt, Publisher.*

Wagner: *Parsifal.*

Dupont: *Poemes d' Automne*

Longer Melodies to Harmonize.

Suggestions:

No. 1. The mediant is useful in harmonizing repetitions of the scale 3rd (Mi).

No. 2. This melody can be harmonized in two ways. First, employ one chord to a measure, except when approaching cadences. Second, harmonize each pulse. Try III at the middle cadence. The last four measures are effectively harmonized by a sequence of 7th chords (all first species). Start the phrase with VI7.

No. 6. Notice the melodic sequence. Employ a harmonic sequence.

No. 7. Divide the first phrase into sections, a and a'. Try primary harmonies in section a, and substitutional harmonies in a'. The same plan may be used later in the melody.

No. 8. The sequence is effective with primary and substitutional harmonies.

No. 9. Refer to Chapter XIII, Ex. 158, for discussion of the phrase cadence of this melody

No. 13. Refer to the Beethoven excerpt, No. 8 of the Analysis, for a suggested bass.

No. 14. Try I - III7 - vi for the first three notes of bar three.

No. 15. Note the $\overset{5}{\text{irregular}}$ form as diagrammed:

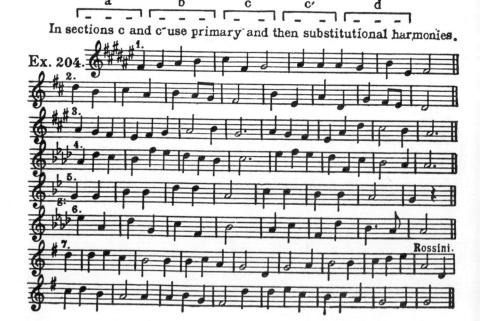

Chapter XVII.

Modulation.

Play the following example. In the section marked (b) notice that the tone center has changed from C to G.

Shifting the tone center, or moving from one key into another, is called *modulation*.

At times, what appears to be a modulation is in reality only a chromatic progression in the original key.

An *altered or chromatic chord* is one which contains one or more tones foreign to the scale, without effecting a modulation. If the harmony following the altered chord is in the same key as that preceding it, there is no modulation, and the altered chord is regarded as chromatic in that key. If the harmony following the altered chord leads to a cadence in another key, modulation is effected and the altered chord is not considered chromatic, but becomes a diatonic chord of the new key:

In the foregoing example, at (a) the altered D chord suggests the dominant-7th chord of the key of G; but the following cadence defines the key of C, consequently there is no modulation, and the D chord is the supertonic-7th, a chromatic imitation of the dominant-7th. At (b) the harmony following the D chord unmistakably establishes the key of G, so the D chord is considered a dominant-7th of the key of G in which it is diatonic.

Key is the result of relationship and no single chord can establish it except the *second inversion* of an *accented major or minor triad* which asserts itself as a new tonic.

Note how Wagner *affirms* each new key by a second inversion (I_5) and *confirms* the modulation by using V-I.

Wagner: *Lohengrin*

Ex. 207.

D: I_5 F:

I_5 Ab I_5

The simplest modulations are to the keys whose tonics are distant a perfect fifth or perfect fourth. The nearest related keys to any major key are its *dominant, subdominant* and *relative minor*. These keys have signatures which differ from the signature of the original key by not more than one sharp or one flat. Ex. 208. Each of these related keys has six tones in common with the original key.

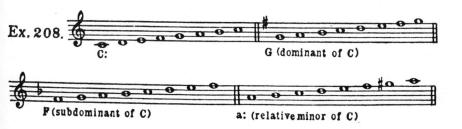

Ex. 208.

C: G (dominant of C)

F (subdominant of C)   a: (relative minor of C)

Modulation to the Dominant Key.

An excellent method of modulation to the dominant key is accomplished by affirming the new key with the *accented* second inversion of its tonic chord (I). In a four measure phrase this usually occurs on the accent of measure three. The I of the new key is best approached by IV or ii, those chords being I and vi, respectively, in the original key. Refer again to Ex 205 and confirm the preceding statements.

A modulation is said to be *complete* when the new key is confirmed with both rhythmic and harmonic cadence.

When approaching the new key, avoid the use of a tone that will re-affirm the old key. For example: when moving from the key of C to the key of G, avoid chords which contain F, as that tone suggests the old key.

On general principles, the affirmation of a new key is not heard until the *cadence section*. The return to the tonic key is usually at the beginning of the phrase instead of the close. The V 7 chord of the original key will most definitely reaffirm that key.

Apply the above principles in the following melodies.

Ex. 209.

Another way of entering the new key is thru the V₇ chord. It is best to establish the tonic, then enter the new key thru its V₇ chord *on a weak pulse.*

Play the following pattern in many keys, modulating to the dominant as indicated. Avoid root positions of the V₇ except preceding the final I.

Modulation to the Subdominant Key.

It is difficult to modulate to the subdominant key thru I. In the following melodies, enter the subdominant key thru its V_7 chord, preferably on a weak pulse. The V_7 of the subdominant key is $I\flat_7$ in the original key. Employ inversions as often as possible *except when confirming the cadence.*

Ex. 211.

Keyboard Practice.

1. Employ the pattern of Ex. 210 for modulation to the subdominant key.

2. Employ Ex. 210 modulating to the dominant key. Using the same pattern, return to the original key, this being a subdominant modulation.

Modulation to the Relative Minor.

There are several comparatively simple ways of modulating to the relative minor key:

1. Employ vi as a new tonic. Ex. 212 (a).

2. Employ vii° as ii° in the new key and progress to I. Ex. 212 (b).

3. Enter the new key thru its V_7 (this is III_7 in the original key). Ex. 212 (c).

Ex. 212.

vi = i

(Bb: vii°₃
g: ii°₅)

e: V7

Melodies containing modulations to the relative minor.

Ex. 213.

Keyboard Practice.

1. Employ the pattern of Ex. 210 for modulation to the relative minor. Using the same pattern, return to the original key.

2. Extemporize chorales in four phrase form, making modulations as indicated in the following diagram:

Ex. 214.   A   B   C   D

A—First phrase in original key closing on I.

B—Modulate to the dominant key in the second section (✱).

C—Starting with I of the original key, modulate to the relative minor key in the second section (✩).

D—Starting with V of the original key, return and close with a perfect cadence. If the last phrase starts with an anacrusis, use V at that point.

Analysis.

The new key is generally considered from the beginning of a phrase or section. For example, in the excerpt from Handel, there is nothing to indicate a change of key until the G♮ appears, but the entire phrase should be considered in the key of B minor. Note the means of modulating in the other excerpts.

Ex. 215.

The use of a tetrachord which includes decisive material of the new key is very effective:

Excellent material for analysis of simple modulations is found in the Bach-Album, Vol. 12, published by G. Schirmer, N. Y. C.

Chapter XVIII.

Modulation (continued).

Modulating to unrelated keys, the change is sometimes smoother by passing through another related key.

Observe that the tonal relation of scale applies to key relationship. In Ex. 216, E♭ is IV of B♭. Melodically, C, the scale-2nd, would naturally be taken on the way from scale-4 down to tonic, just as Beethoven chose the keys.

As IV does not contain "Ti,' scale-7th, the use of it does not confirm the key as well as V 7. If it is necessary to employ it, make up the lack in quality by quantity. The melody by Reinecke, No. 3 of Ex. 217, illustrates this. For the return to the key of G at bar nine, IV-I is repeated in the next section. This little melody is very interesting. The first section requires the three primary harmonies, I-IV-V-I. The employment of their substitutes in the next section provides a pleasing contrast, and by the repetition of those harmonies in the third section, the key of e is confirmed. This unifies the work, because these harmonies are primary in the key of e, and the melody, which is the same as the first section, is harmonized in the same way. The next two bars (7th and 8th) may be in the key of D. In its relation to the original key of G, e is the scale-6th, the natural resolution being *down* to D, and the resolution of D *up* to G. Notice the rhythmic proportion of keys.

Usually, the first two bars of the phrase in the new key are made of material common to both keys, the confirmation of the new key falling in the cadence section, as mentioned before. In No. 2 of Ex. 217 the melody modulates in the first section of the second phrase. In that case, it is in good taste to use substitutional chords for the next, or a passing modulation on the way to the old key. That is much better than to reaffirm the transient key.

Melodies with changes of key require less variety of harmonic treatment.

Do not forget to make the changes of key coincident with the rhythmic groups.

There is one important thing that the student *must* remember: *The tones peculiar to the new key should not be introduced before the chords affirm or confirm the new key.*

CHAPTER XIX

Creative Work
COMPOSITIONAL TECHNIQUES

Analyze the form and make diagrams of the melodies of Ex. 217. These melodies illustrate most of the smaller musical forms. For example: No. 1 consists of two periods which are parallel or similar in construction except at the cadences. No. 2 is an example of the "Three-Phrase-Group," A-B-C. No. 3 is a Three-Phrase Group with a short extension. No. 5 illustrates a very small "binary" (two-part) form of two periods, the second period being a development of the material of the first period. No. 14 is a small "ternary" (three-part) form in which Part I is a repeated phrase, Part II a phrase which modulates to the dominant key, and Part III a repetition of the first phrase. No. 15 can be considered a binary form: Part I=a double period; Part II=a group of phrases. No. 16 is a ternary form, slightly more extended than No. 14.

Using the diagrams as models, extemporize and write original compositions. Op. 68 of Schumann will suggest various types of accompaniment and pianistic style. In every case, plan the cadences and modulations first, leaving details until later.

In the larger forms, unless there is some figural work, the first four bar phrase is generally in the tonic key. It is easier to modulate if the first phrase closes with a tonic chord; as it suggests a completed idea, one anticipates a new key for the next cadence.

It has been said that it is vastly more important and effective to employ various inversions and chord positions than many harmonies. On the same principle, it is more important that one should learn to use the various harmonies skilfully than it is to modulate frequently, the latter being the resort of the unskilful. Unless the idea to be expressed requires a change of key to one better suited, there should be no modulation.

In key relation, the subdominant key is retrospective; for that reason it is not likely to be employed for the first change of key. In a Ternary form, the third part is quite likely to be in the subdominant key, and in sonatas, one hears it in the recapitulation, possibly in the development group.

A certain amount of preparation at the keyboard is not only legitimate but desirable. Every composition should be carefully examined *away* from the piano, however, as too great reliance upon the help of an instrument leads to careless habits. Not every student is a potential composer, but the rhythmic-melodic-harmonic vocabulary should be employed in as creative a manner as possible.

The melodies in Example 217 can be employed as basic material for larger forms. For example, No. 11 can be extended to a small ternary form by writing a middle section and adding a short coda. In small forms Part II is quite often a development of the material in Part I, rather than a decided contrast. In the following illustration note the imitative figures, both tonal and rhythmic, and observe that the added section is based to a considerable extent on the original material. Amplifying and developing in this manner is an excellent means of preparing for entirely original work.

Exercises in compositional techniques of
various periods in the history of music.

The following exercises in compositional techniques present a miniature panorama of the styles employed over a period extending from 1600 to the present day. Naturally, this brief survey is necessarily cursory and serves merely as an introduction to the different technical procedures.

In some cases the student is "guided" to a very considerable extent by the suggestions and the figuring. In other examples he is left relatively free to experiment within the particular technique indicated.

With the exception of the Brahms and Elgar excerpts, examples from the romantic period are not given for two reasons. First, the text itself includes a large number of melodies and basses from composers of this era. Second, the romantic period abounds in chromatic harmonies which have been discussed only in an incidental manner. The theory and practice of chromatic harmony are discussed thoroughly in Part II.

The examples of Caccini, Peri and Monteverdi consist almost entirely of triads in root position with an occasional chord of the sixth (first inversion) and incidental use of suspensions and ritardations, although one excerpt from Monteverdi includes "prepared sevenths." The music from the Baroque period displays more florid basses and is contrapuntal although based on harmonic progressions. The examples of Haydn and Mozart are more harmonic and the bass parts are less complicated than those of Bach and Handel.

Several exercises in contemporary techniques are given since the material consists largely of triads and the student is quite capable of manipulating this material as indicated. He will be more interested perhaps in these harmonic combinations than in the technical procedures of the romantic era.

In addition to working out the exercises, the student is advised to look up the composers and the works given and to compare his versions with the originals.

Fill in the voices of the following figured bass and melody from the early opera, *L'Euridice* by Caccini.

Ex. 219

Caccini *L'Euridice (1600)*

Complete the following excerpt.

Ex. 220

Peri: *L'Euridice (1600)*

Complete the following example from Monteverdi's important opera *Orfeo.*

Ex. 221   Monteverdi *Orfeo* (*1607*)

Sinfonia

The following passage from Monteverdi's *Combattimento di Tancredi e Clorinda* consists largely of secondary seventh chords. Continue the pattern indicated in the first measure.

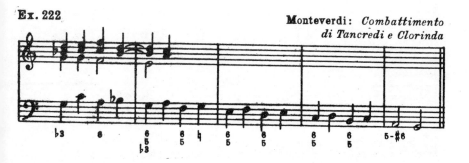

Ex. 222   Monteverdi: *Combattimento di Tancredi e Clorinda*

In the following melody which is an area from a solo cantata by Cesti, employ the type of accompaniment suggested and complete the exercise.

Ex. 223

Cesti (1620-1669): Aria from *La Corte di Roma*

In the following passage from a harpsichord suite by Purcell, complete as follows: (1) in measures two and three imitate the melody shown in measure one (2) in measure six, imitate the upper voice exactly (3) in measures 9-10 fill in the voices and add a figure in the bass of the final measure.

Ex. 224

Purcell: *Prelude-Suite for harpsichord*

Complete the following exercise which is patterned on the style of J. S. Bach. In the second phrase it is not necessary to imitate all the figures, especially when approaching the cadence.

Ex. 225

Complete the following passage from the *Brandenburg Concerto* No. 2 in F major (Mov. 2). Employ figures from the material given, using two and three voices. Note the modulations to the dominant (A minor) and its relative major (C). The excerpt given closes in the dominant key, but interested students should compare with the complete score.

Ex. 226

Andante   J. S. Bach: *Brandenburg Concerto No. 2, Mov. 2*

Complete the melody from Handel's opera *Rodelinda*, using the type of accompaniment suggested in the first four measures. Observe the figuring indicated.

Ex. 227   Handel: *Rodelinda, No. 7 (Arietta)*

Complete the recitative preceding the tenor air "In native worth" from Haydn's oratorio *The Creation*. Attempt to reflect the meaning of the text by using appropriate leaps. It will be necessary to use eighth and sixteenth notes at several places.

Fill in the harmony above the figured bass.

Ex. 228

Haydn: *The Creation*
Recit. -"And God created Man"

And God cre-a-ted | Man in His own | image, In the image of

God cre-a-ted he him; | Male and female cre-a-ted he them. He breath-ed

in-to his nostrils the breath of | life, and | Man be- | came a living soul.

Harmonize the air which follows the above recitative. Only the first twelve measures are given. There is one chord with which the student may not be familiar since it has not been discussed in previous chapters. This chord is figured $\frac{6+}{3}$ and leads to the $\frac{6}{4}$ in the cadence. The chord is a minor subdominant in first inversion with the root sharped (the chromatic tone is in the melody in this example). The chord is called an *augmented six-three* and often referred to as the "Italian Sixth."

Detailed explanation will be found in *Applied Harmony*, Part II.

Ex. 229   Haydn: *The Creation*
     Air - "In native worth"

In   na - tive worth and   hon - or clad, With beau - ty, cour - age,

strength a-dorn'd, E - rect with front se - rene   He   stands,   A

Man,   the   Lord   and   King   of   na - ture all.

To aid the student the *augmented six-three* or "Italian Sixth" is illustrated here.

After the student has completed the preceding recitative and air, he should examine the score and ascertain how closely he has approximated the original.

Harmonize the melody from Mozart's *Il Seraglio*, a difficult aria sung by Constanze. Note that the florid passages are harmonized with fewer chords.

Ex. 230

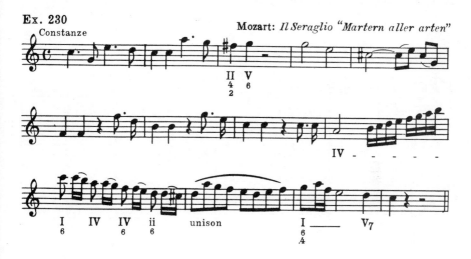

Mozart: *Il Seraglio "Martern aller arten"*

Harmonize the following melody employing a simple form of accompaniment based on models from works of Mozart illustrated in the text.

Ex. 231

Mozart: *The Magic Flute*

The above excerpt is from a duet sung by Pamina (soprano) and Papageno (baritone).

In the following, treat the excerpt as a "bass melody," not as the real bass of the harmony. Employ the accompaniment figure indicated. This noble melody is sung by the high priest, Sarastro(bass).

Ex. 232
Sarastro

Mozart: *The Magic Flute,* "*O Isis und Osiris*"

Melody continued

C: ii   V

g:

i   F: V₇

ii   vi
6

Harmonize the chorale melody by Haydn which Brahms used for his famous orchestral variations. The form is a small ternary in which Part I consists of two five measure phrases, Part II of two four measure phrases and Part III (curtailed) repeats the first phrase. A short codetta is added in which the I♭₇ and IV should be employed. The diagram will clarify the form, which is a combination of the traditional and the unusual.

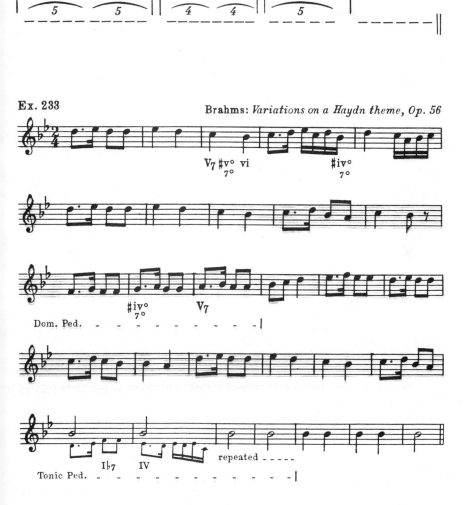

Ex. 233   Brahms: *Variations on a Haydn theme, Op. 56*

The above theme is usually called the "Saint Anthony Chorale."

Complete the following exercise which is the theme from Elgar's *Enigma Variations* for orchestra, Op. 36. Fill in the inner voices according to the figured bass. In several cases the inner voices are added as it is difficult to indicate the contrapuntal lines from the figures. After completion the student should compare his solution with the original score. Note the "tierce de Picardie" at the final cadence. The form of the theme is a miniature *ternary*.

Ex. 234
Andante   **Elgar:** Theme from *Enigma Variations Op. 36*

Exercises in the contemporary idiom

Harmonize the following melody with i (minor) and IV (major) only. The cadence can be either i or IV. Bartok closes on the D major chord and thus creates a modal effect.

Ex. 235   Bartok   *Little Pieces for Children, Vol I, No. 3*

    i   IV₉   i   IV   i   IV

Harmonize the following melody in the style indicated. Notice that the dominant harmony is employed only in the second phrase, except the one minor dominant (v) in measure 14. Close with the major tonic (I).

Ex. 236

etc.

Melody continued

    iv   iv₇   i — v   iv   ♯iv   i   iv+6   I

Harmonize the next melody with *major chords only*, as indicated, using the spacing shown in measure one. This harmonic relation of roots (a minor third above and below a tonic) is often found in contemporary music.

Ex. 237

    G: Bb: G: G: E: G:

In the following exercise, continue the sequence until the final cadence is reached. A major chord is followed by a minor chord built on the small third (or augmented second) above. The root of this chord is held over as the fifth of the next major chord. The effect of this passage is quite "modern" although not dissonant.

Ex. 238

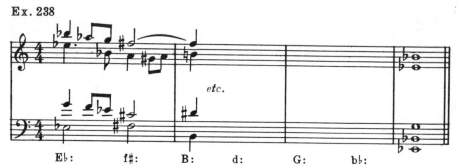

In the melody from *The King's Henchman*, the opera by Deems Taylor, note the suggestions for use of the minor dominant (v) and the "parallel" progression of i - ♭VII-VI in measures 5-6 and 8-9.

Ex. 239

"Oh,Caesar, great wert thou."   Taylor: *The King's Henchman*

By permission of J. Fischer and Bro., copyright owner.

The student who has carefully worked out the preceding exercises should now be ready to experiment "on his own," composing short works in various of the small forms already discussed and employing the harmonic material outlined in the text.

As stated several times previously, composition cannot be "taught" but inspiration may be "caught" by analyzing the works of great composers, observing the forms and the technical processes they employ.

APPENDIX

Chapter I.

Consecutive First Inversions of Triads.

The problem of consecutive first inversions of triads has been left until this point because such passages are comparatively rare and the technique involved is concerned primarily with avoidance of fifths and octaves. In preceding lessons there have been examples of two or more first inversions in succession, but more extended passages require further discussion, and more drill on the part of the student. The problem is largely contrapuntal, and if the voices are manipulated properly, the triads need not progress in the so-called "natural" order. In the following passage the triads are on adjacent degrees of the scale. Note the *symmetrical doubling* at (a) where the root and third are doubled in alternate chords. It is possible to move the voices as shown at (b) and (c). In these cases observe that the root, third, or fifth is doubled according to the movement of the parts.

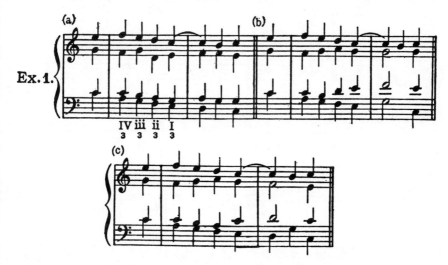

Symmetrical doubling is preferable in sequences, as illustrated in the following:

Add the inner parts to the following exercises. Double the root, third, or fifth in major and minor triads. In the case of vii° and III+, avoid doubling the leading tone, except in a sequence.

In No. 2 add an alto part in constant quarter notes.

Analyze the following, noting the doubling, movement of voices and the employment of short rhythmic figures which serve as unifying elements.

Construct similar exercises in both modes, using sequences and free patterns of triads in first inversion.

*The fifths between alto and tenor, moving by half step, are not objectionable.

Melodies to Harmonize.

In addition to the chords marked, employ first inversions at *.

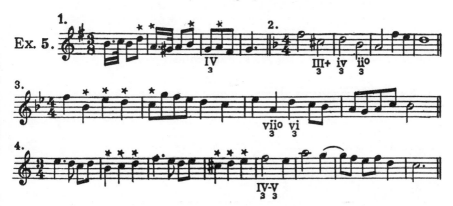

Harmonize number 5 in the *natural minor*, except at the cadence.

Chapter II.

Secondary Seventh Chords.

All seventh chords except the dominant-seventh are called secondary (or collateral) sevenths. Those on the tonic and subdominant (major mode) include the interval of a large seventh, while the ii7, iii7, and vi7 have small sevenths. The vii°7 also contains a small seventh. This chord, as mentioned in Chapter IX, is often classified as an incomplete V⁹.

Ex. 6.

    I7   IV7   ii7   iii7   vi7   vii°7

Compare the above seventh chords with those of the minor mode. Three new structures occur, two very dissonant chords on the tonic and the mediant, and a diminished seventh on the subtonic (this chord, vii°7°, is discussed at length in Applied Harmony, Part II).

Ex. 7.

    i7   ii°7   III+7   iv7   VI7   vii°7°

The seventh undoubtedly originated as a passing tone from the octave. Since the interval of a seventh is dissonant, the early contrapuntists treated it as a suspension, preparing the dissonance and resolving it by step, as illustrated in the following:

Bonadies (1473)
Kyrie

Ex. 8.

When the theory of triads, seventh chords, and their inversions was established,[1] the preparation of the chord-seventh was usually required and its normal resolution was downward by step. The masters of the 18th century observed this rule of preparation and resolution more often than they ignored it. The seventh was not always prepared in the same voice, as illustrated by the Rameau excerpt. The seventh of the supertonic (measure two) is prepared by the last bass note of the preceding measure.

Rameau: *La poule.*

Ex. 9.

---

1. Principally by Rameau in his notable treatise, Traité de l'Harmonie (1722)

Ex. 10 illustrates a sequence of prepared sevenths. Note that in the first seventh chord the fifth is omitted and the root doubled, while the following chord is complete. This is frequently the case in sequences of this type. In both examples the resolution is stepwise.

The student should analyze the following very carefully, as examples of secondary seventh chords:

Bach: Prelude Number 1, Well Tempered Clavichord, Book I.

Schumann: "Ich grolle nicht." In this example the sevenths are apparently approached by a wide leap, but in reality the resolution merely takes place in a higher register.

Grieg: Op. 40, "Aus Holberg's Zeit."

Debussy: "The maid with the flaxen hair."

In the following sequence the seventh of each chord enters by step, but instead of resolving, it is prolonged into the succeeding chord.

In the first measure of the foregoing example the bass and soprano move in similar motion to a seventh. Many older texts object to such a progression, but it is found in music literature of widely separated epochs.

Write and play the following sequences, preparing each chord-seventh or allowing it to enter stepwise, and resolving the seventh down one degree.

1. I₃ I7₃ vii° vii⁷₃ vi₃ vi7 etc.

2. I vii⁹₃ - iii7 vi7₃ ii7 V7 I

3. I I7₃ IV vii⁹₃ iii vi7 ii V7 I

4. I I IV7 vii° iii⁷ vi ii7 V I V7 I

Irregular Resolutions.

The seventh need not resolve down by step. It may move up or down by degree or may leap. The seventh may also be approached by leap, or, in other words, it may enter *unprepared*.

Gabriel Fauré is especially interesting in his treatment of seventh chords. His manner of writing increased in freedom. Starting somewhat tentatively, he eventually reached a state of dissonance which is quite daring, considering the general reticence of his style. The following excerpts present a miniature summary of this evolution.

Harmonize the following melodies, employing secondary sevenths and their inversions. Use both prepared and unprepared sevenths, and practice the conventional resolutions as well as the irregular. Employ seventh chords at *. Additional exercises (figured basses) will be found in the following chapter.

The following excerpts illustrate the free use of seventh chords. Debussy, Satie, Ravel, and other composers of the French school in particular, employ sevenths in parallel motion. This technique, strangely enough, is anticipated by earlier composers, as shown by the Pasquini example.

At the time when the composers mentioned were experimenting with seventh chords in the most radical manner, the French theorists[1] of the day continued to prohibit the unprepared seventh and to restrict its resolution, but the old rules are practically discarded today. It is possible to make but a few generalizations. In the stricter type of vocal (choral) composition one observes adherence to the rules, but modern composers employ seventh chords in writing for voices with almost as much freedom as in the instrumental field. When the seventh is approached by a wide leap—in the bass—it is striking enough in its effect to require some discretion as to its frequent use. The second inversion is relatively rare and the seventh is usually prepared. The best advice for the student is to analyze many examples and trust to the aural discrimination which results from contact with good models. Writing original phrases which include secondary seventh chords will accomplish more than the harmonization of melodies and basses.

1. Reicha, Bazin, Reber, etc.

Chapter III.

The Figured Bass.

The figured bass is a system which indicates harmonic relations above a given bass part.   While it was originally employed merely to avoid the labor of writing out the complete harmonies and to serve as a guide to the accompanist who played from a single bass part, it gradually became the basis for a method of teaching harmony.

The invention of the figured bass (called *basso continuo* by the composers of the 17th and 18th centuries) is popularly attributed to Ludovico Viadana (1564-1645), although some writers claim that his use of figures to indicate the harmony was anticipated a few years prior to 1605, the date usually given. Carl von Winterfeld[1] claims that Viadana was not the inventor of the system, but that Peri's *Euridice* contains figured bass.   Considerably before the time of Winterfeld, John Hawkins[2] called attention to the fact that in Richard Deering's *Cantiones Sacrae* (1597) the bass is figured with a 6 whenever that concord appears.   This idea was repeated by several writers, but has not been accepted by all.   Robert Eitner[3] in his Quellen-Lexikon doubts the authenticity of the statement.   It appears that the exact date or absolute certainty as to the priority of the use of figured bass can scarcely be established.

The essential tones of the chord are indicated by the figures below the given bass.   By finding the intervals above the bass part the student can determine the chords to be employed.   This process can be done mechanically with no concept of the harmonic relations involved; but it is far better for the student to learn the relation of the figures to the chords and their inversions as already known.   The following illustrates the figuring for triads and seventh chords.   The absence of a figure indicates that a triad is to be used.

The figuring for seventh chords is often abbreviated, especially the second inversion, which appears as $\frac{4}{3}$, and the third inversion which is written $\frac{4}{2}$, and sometimes 2.

In working out the following basses, the student is advised to determine the chords by means of the figures, then to write the other parts by following principles of spacing, doubling, voice leading, etc., as learned in preceding lessons.   The process of harmonization is not different from that which has been discussed in the text; the problem is merely that of finding the correct chords by means of a figuring which is relatively unfamiliar.

1. Johannes Gabrieli und sein Zeitalter (1834) Part II, p. 59.
2. An Inquiry in the Nature and Principles of Thorough Bass (1817) p. 22.
3. Op. cit. (1900) p. 162.

Ex. 18 illustrates a bass and two examples of how it may be worked out. The figures do not indicate the arrangement of voices above the bass; this is left to the discretion of the student. Occasionally a figure is placed above the bass to indicate a particular chord degree for the melody.

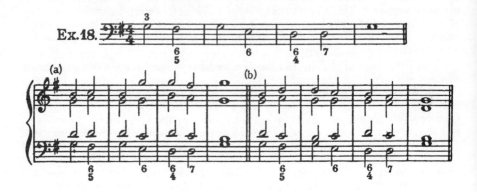

Basses employing primary chords and their inversions.

In the minor mode, the harmonic form of the scale is presupposed unless otherwise indicated. A ♯ or ♮ under a bass note indicates that the third above that note is to be major. This usually occurs with the V chord.

Ex. 20 illustrates the figuring for suspensions and ritardations.

Basses employing secondary harmonies and bytones.

Figured bass from a Concerto Ecclesiastico by Viadana.

Basses from Chorales of J. S. Bach.

INDEX

The numbers refer to pages.